7/17

ISLINGTON

Please return this item on or before the last date stamped below or you may be liable to overdue charges. To renew an item call the number below, or access the online catalogue at www.islington.gov.uk/libraries. You will need your library membership number and PIN number.

1 4 MAR 2018

2 2 NOV 2019

Islington Libraries

020 7527 6900 ~~www.islington.gov.uk/~~braries

D1464394

1917

Stories and Poems from the Russian Revolution

Selected by Boris Dralyuk

PUSHKIN PRESS

Pushkin Press
71–75 Shelton Street, London WC2H 9JQ

1917: Stories and Poems from the Russian Revolution first published in 2016

9 8 7 6 5 4 3 2 1

ISBN 978 1 782272 14 4

Text designed and set in Monotype Dante by Teragon, London
Printed by CPI Group (UK) Ltd, Croydon, CRO 4YY

www.pushkinpress.com

Contents

Editor's Note

The pieces I've chosen for this collection were written between February 1917, when the revolutionary forces in Petrograd and Moscow toppled the Romanov dynasty, and late 1919, when the Bolsheviks, who had seized power on 25 October (7 November, NS) 1917, finally turned the tide against the White Army in the Russian Civil War of 1917–21. The rationale for limiting the anthology's scope to these two and a half years was simple: My aim was not so much to tell the story of the revolutionary period as to steep the reader in its tumult—to recreate the heady brew of enthusiasm and disgust, passion and trepidation that intoxicated Russia and the world as the events unfolded. Consequently, I wanted to avoid memoirs and retrospective works of fiction, as well as commemorative poems, of which there is no dearth. These backward-looking works, be they written from a Soviet or anti-Soviet perspective, treat the revolutions and the Civil War as a single *fait accompli*, a decisive but entirely decided matter. Many important longer works are also readily available in stand-alone translations; I draw on and point to these works in the introductory notes to the anthology's subsections.

As for the story of the Russian Revolution, it has been told many times. In English, it has been covered especially well by Orlando Figes, Sheila Fitzpatrick and Robert Service, and this anthology may be read alongside their volumes. Since my target audience is English-speaking, I have tried to use English-language sources in my notes whenever possible.

The first part of the collection, 'The Revolution: A Poem-Chronicle', takes its title from a long poem by Vladimir Mayakovsky (see pp. 68–70), written in the month or so following the February Revolution, in which the poet declares:

> The courses of planets,
> the existence of states:
> all are subordinate to our wills.
> The earth is ours.
> The air is ours.
> Ours is the diamond mine of the stars.
> And we will never—
> no, we will never!—
> permit a soul—
> no, not a soul!—
> to tear at our earth with cannon balls,
> to pierce our air with the points of spears.
>
> *(Translated by James Womack)*

Mayakovsky's radical prediction that the events of February would bring about lasting peace was, of course, proved tragically wrong. The Provisional Government refused to withdraw Russian troops from the First World War, a fact the Bolsheviks used to justify their takeover in October. And though the Bolsheviks did secure a peace with the Central Powers at Brest-Litovsk on 3 March 1918, their coup plunged Russia into a protracted civil war, with Russia's former allies— including the French, the British and the Americans—intervening on behalf of the White opposition. The combination of passionate idealism and tragic misapprehension in Mayakovsky's poem lends it great poignancy. His "poem-chronicle" could not have been written in the 1920s, after the dust of 1917 had settled. I feel the same can be said of most of the poems I have selected for my "poem-chronicle". They are grouped in six sections, each linked by a common theme, attitude or striking image. The introductions are brief, and anyone wishing to learn about the lives of most of these poets and to read more of their work may consult *The Penguin Book of Russian Poetry* (2015), edited by Robert Chandler, Irina Mashinski and myself.

The second part of the collection is devoted to prose, and it too is separated into sections linked by theme or some other unexpected commonality. The introductions to these sections are more substantial, providing fuller biographical sketches of the authors, many of whom are little known in the English-speaking world, and some of whom are almost forgotten even in Russia. I have also included one story translated from the Yiddish of Dovid Bergelson, as well as a poem translated from the Georgian of Titsian Tabidze; the events of 1917 affected all the peoples of the Russian Empire, and had I the space, I would have included pieces translated from Estonian, Latvian, Lithuanian, Polish, Ukrainian and the languages of Central Asia. Had I more space yet, I would have included works by authors from around the globe, since the days of 1917 did indeed, to paraphrase John Reed, shake the world.

Much of my work on this anthology was done in Scotland, and I would like to illustrate the riches I have had to exclude for reasons of language, geography and chronology by quoting Hugh MacDiarmid's (1892–1978) electrifying quatrain 'The Skeleton of the Future (At Lenin's Tomb)', written in the early 1930s:

> Red granite and black diorite, with the blue
> Of the labradorite crystals gleaming like precious stones
> In the light reflected from the snow; and behind them
> The eternal lightning of Lenin's bones.

Acknowledgements

I must thank Adam Freudenheim, Gesche Ipsen and Julia Nicholson at Pushkin Press, for commissioning me to work on this dream of a project and for all the support and encouragement they have given me along the way. I owe a great debt to the brilliant translators who have contributed their talents to this anthology: Josh Billings, Maria Bloshteyn, Michael Casper, Robert Chandler, Peter France, Rose France, Lisa Hayden, Bryan Karetnyk, Martha Kelly, Donald Rayfield, Margo Shohl Rosen and James Womack. It is my honour to foreground their work, and I am just as honoured to reintroduce the work of translators who are no longer with us: Mirra Ginsburg, Jack Lindsay, Alex Miller, Gerard Shelley and Jon Stallworthy. I am deeply grateful for the help and advice of my colleagues Emily Finer, Victoria Donovan, Katharine Holt, Olga Voronina and Claire Whitehead of the University of St Andrews, and Yelena Furman, Georgiana Galateanu, Olga Kagan, Susan Kresin, Gail Lenhoff, Lada Panova and Ronald Vroon of UCLA. I am especially grateful to Sean Griffin, Roman Koropeckyj and Michael Lavery of UCLA, who—quite characteristically—went above and beyond the call of collegial duty. An event dedicated to this anthology at Pushkin House in London in October 2015, organized by Ursula Woolley, brought together an extraordinarily informed audience, including the poets

D.M. Black, Stephan Capus, Peter Daniels and Stephen Watts, who made invaluable comments on the works I presented. Edythe Haber, an expert on Teffi, helped me sort out some mysteries regarding that author's work. I have saved my final tip of the hat for the remarkably knowledgeable and perceptive Stephen Dodson, whose sharp eyes have rescued me from myriad blunders. Needless to say, the blame for all remaining blunders lies with me.

I would like to dedicate this anthology to the memory of my grandmother, Yekaterina Pavlovskaya, who was a two-year-old girl in Odessa when the Bolsheviks seized power in Petrograd in 1917, and who outlived the Soviet Union by twenty-one years.

THE REVOLUTION

A Poem-Chronicle

STOLEN WINE

In 1917 Maxim Gorky (1868–1936), a friend of Vladimir Lenin's since 1907, began to publish a series of articles in the Petrograd daily *Novaya Zhizn* (*New Life*), raising serious questions about the behaviour of the Russian masses during that revolutionary year and, most daringly, about Bolshevik policy after the seizure of power in October. These "untimely thoughts" established Gorky, a committed Marxist, as "the conscience of the revolution". On 7 December 1917, Gorky complained:

> Every night for almost two weeks crowds of people have been robbing wine cellars, getting drunk, banging each other over the head with bottles, cutting their hands with fragments of glass, and wallowing like pigs in filth and blood. Over this period, wine worth several tens of millions of rubles has been destroyed, and, of course, hundreds of millions of rubles' worth will continue to be destroyed.

Russians had lived under a limited dry law since the beginning of the First World War. Did they really desire political freedom or merely a drunken free-for-all? Gorky wasn't the only one to sense the deeper implications of this looting. Depictions of the "wine riots" run like a red stream through the work of monarchist and liberal diarists, memoirists and authors recoiling from the chaos of 1917. The organs of Bolshevik propaganda laid the blame for the riots squarely at the feet of the bourgeoisie, and the new government's international supporters helped spread that message far and wide. In his slanted but marvellously evocative *Through the Russian Revolution* (1921), Albert Rhys Williams toed the party line:

> In their efforts to befuddle the brains of the masses the bourgeoisie saw an ally in alcohol. The city was mined with wine cellars more dangerous than powder magazines. This alcohol in the veins of the populace meant chaos in the life of the city. With this aim the cellars were opened and the mob invited in to help themselves. Bottles in hand the drunks would emerge from the cellars to fall sprawling on the snow, or rove thru the streets, shooting and looting.
>
> To these pogroms the Bolsheviks replied with machine-guns, pouring lead into the bottles—there was no time to break them all by hand. They destroyed three million rubles' worth of vintage in the vaults of the Winter Palace, some of it there for a century. The liquor passed out of the cellars, not thru the throats of the Czar and his retainers, but thru a hose attached to a fire-engine pumping into the canals. A frightful loss. The Bolsheviks deeply regretted it, for they needed funds. But they needed order more.

Gorky, for his part, saw through all this: "*Pravda* writes about the drunken riots as a 'provocation of the bourgeoisie' which, of course, is a lie, an 'eloquent phrase' that can increase bloodshed." Propaganda notwithstanding, the sight of drunken burghers, peasants and soldiers—of wine mingling with blood—left an enormous impression on all those who lived through those days.

The young Marina Tsvetaeva, who would eventually emerge as one of the major poets of the twentieth century, taps into this current in a riveting poem set in the Crimean port of Feodosia—the half-sprung, half-reeling rhythm of her verse providing a perfect formal analogue to its apocalyptic themes and imagery. Beneath the poem, she added: "NB! The birds were drunk." It is drawn from a collection that Tsvetaeva completed but didn't publish during her lifetime, *The Demesne of Swans*, in which, as Peter France writes, "she praised the nobility of those who died for the anti-revolutionary cause. They are swans, white and pure, against the ravens." But with Tsvetaeva things were never quite so simple. France continues: "There is no doubt about Tsvetaeva's position at this time, but equally there is no doubt that her heart went out above all to the gallant loser, the victim."

In his study of the poet, Simon Karlinsky explains her shifting allegiances throughout the year—she dedicated poems to Tsar Nicholas II after his abdication, but also wrote a poem to Alexander Kerensky, the leader of the Provisional Government, in which she compares him, favourably, to Napoleon, and a sequence valorizing the seventeenth-century rebel Stenka Razin: "Her basic humanity invariably led Tsvetaeva to take the side of the underdog, which for her meant any individual of whatever station who was threatened by a dehumanized collective, be it a mob, a political party or the state." Owing partly to this idiosyncratic stance and to the formally "revolutionary" nature of her poetics, Tsvetaeva never felt at home among the émigrés in Paris, where she finally settled in 1925, after leaving Soviet Russia in 1922 and spending some time in Berlin and Prague. Writing to a Czech friend in 1929, she complained that, "For those on the Right—[my work] is 'left' in form. For those on the Left—it is 'right' in content." A decade later, Tsvetaeva returned to the Soviet Union, following her husband Sergey Efron, a former White officer who had begun working for the NKVD (the Soviet secret police), and daughter Ariadna, who shared her father's pro-Soviet views. Not long after Tsvetaeva's arrival, Efron and Ariadna were arrested for espionage; Efron was executed in 1941 and Ariadna was sentenced to eight years in prison. Emotionally devastated and lacking any means of support, Tsvetaeva hanged herself on 31 August 1941.

The older Symbolist Zinaida Gippius, who saw the carnage and Bacchanalia around her as a betrayal of the democratic ideals of several generations of Russian freedom fighters, dating back to the Decembrist Uprising of 1825, also seizes on the image of "stolen wine". Both Tsvetaeva and Gippius ponder the nature of the people's new-found freedom: Gippius despairs at what the Russians had done with this Beautiful Lady they had anticipated, while Tsvetaeva, who was wary of the year's revolutionary developments from the start, doubts the Lady was ever who she appeared to be. These poems offer a vivid portrait of the tumult unleashed by the February and October Revolutions, and, in the case of Gippius, the disenchantment they triggered even among those who were eager to see Russia transformed.

MARINA TSVETAEVA (1892–1941)

You stepped from a stately cathedral
onto the blare of the plazas...
—Freedom!—The Beautiful Lady
of Russian grand dukes and marquises.

A fateful choir's rehearsing—
the liturgy still lies before us!
—Freedom!—A street-walking floozy
on the foolhardy breast of a soldier!

26 MAY 1917

(Translated by Boris Dralyuk)

Night.—Northeaster.—Roar of soldiers.—Roar of waves.
Wine cellars raided.—Down every street,
every gutter—a flood, a precious flood,
and in it, dancing, a moon the colour of blood.

Tall poplars stand dazed.
Birds sing all night—crazed.
A tsar's statue—razed,
black night in its place.

Barracks and harbour drink, drink.
The world and its wine—ours!
The town stamps about like a bull,
swills from the turbid puddles.

The moon in a cloud of wine.—Who's that? Stop!
Be my comrade, sweetheart: drink up!
Merry stories go round:
Deep in wine—a couple has drowned.

FEODOSIA, THE LAST DAYS OF OCTOBER 1917

(Translated by Boris Dralyuk)

ZINAIDA GIPPIUS (1869–1945)

Now

> The streets are slippery and vile—
>   disgrace!
> Life is so shameful, so incredible
>   these days!
>
> We all lie bound, bespattered,
>   on every street.
> Our foreheads are all smeared
>   with sailors' spit.
>
> Our guardians and warriors
>   have all retreated.
> There's no one but conformists,
>   with their Committees.
>
> We're all a bunch of homeless curs—
>   completely stranded!
> The Bolsheviks tore up the rails
>   with sooty hands...

9 NOVEMBER, 1917

(Translated by Boris Dralyuk)

What Have We Done to It?

Our grandads' outlandish dream,
the prison years of our heroes,
our lament and our hope,
the prayer we hardly dared utter—
our scuttled, shattered,
Constituent Assembly?

12 NOVEMBER 1917

(Translated by Robert Chandler)

14 December 1917

For Dmitry Merezhkovsky

Will our pure heroes grant us pardon?
We didn't keep their covenant—
all that is holy has been squandered:
our shame, the honour of our land.

We stood beside them, stood together,
when storm clouds gathered in our skies.
The Bride appeared. And then the soldiers
drove bayonets through both her eyes.

We drowned her amid petty quarrels,
in stolen wine, in Palace vats.
The royal axe and noose were cleaner
than these apes' bloodied hands!

Golitsyn, Trubetskoy, Ryleyev!
You've gone now to that far-off land…
Your faces would all blaze with wrath,
seeing the Neva's sullied banks!

From this low pit, this bitter torment,
where acrid smoke circles the depths,
we stretch our trembling arms towards
your distant sacred robes.

To lay hands on those burial garments,
to touch them with our lifeless lips,
to die, or maybe to awaken…
Can't live like this! Can't live like this!

(Translated by Boris Dralyuk)

OSIP MANDELSTAM (1891–1938)

In public and behind closed doors we slowly
    lose our minds,
  and then the brutal winter offers us
  clean, cold Rhine wine.

The chill extends to us, in silver buckets,
    Valhalla's wine,
  which calls to mind the fair-haired image
    of Northern man.

    But Northern skalds are crude,
    don't know the joy of games,
    and Northern warriors are fond
    of amber, feasts and flames.

    They'll never taste the Southern air—
    enchanted foreign skies—
  and so the stubborn maiden
  will refuse their wine.

DECEMBER 1917

(Translated by Boris Dralyuk)

A DISTANT VOICE

With its palpable longing for the gentle air of the Mediterranean—associated with the sustaining, civilizing forces of Western culture—Mandelstam's 'In public and behind closed doors...' is a typically Acmeistic reaction to the upheaval of 1917. The Acmeist group, founded in 1912 by the gallant, adventurous warrior-poet Nikolay Gumilyov (1886–1921) and Sergey Gorodetsky (1884–1967), rejected the mystical vagaries of the preceding generation of Russian poets, emphasizing instead the virtues of clarity, harmony and mastery of technique. Their poetry was, in effect, a turn towards the phenomenal world—the world as it is, not as a sign or symbol of some noumenal realm lying beyond it. As Gorodetsky wrote in one of the movement's earliest manifestos, "For the Acmeists the rose has once again become beautiful in itself, through its petals, scent and colour, and not through its imagined similarities to mystical love or whatever else."

Gumilyov organized a "Guild of Poets", a workshop to develop and spread his poetic principles, and this exclusive milieu fostered two of the most important poetic talents of the twentieth century, Mandelstam and Gumilyov's wife until 1918, Anna Akhmatova. The Acmeists' turn towards the world meant a responsiveness not only to nature, to urban life and to culture, but also to politics. All wrote poems about the First World War, though each from a different perspective: Gumilyov as an officer in the Imperial Army, Akhmatova as a wife on the home front, and Mandelstam as an intellectual grappling with the forces of history. One might have expected the same level of engagement in the aftermath of 1917. Gumilyov, who was stationed abroad in 1917, returned to Soviet Russia in 1918. Although he didn't write overtly political poems, he never hid his monarchist views or his allegiance to the Orthodox faith. His avoidance of politics in his poetry didn't save him; he was arrested on 3 August 1921, accused of participating in an anti-government plot, and executed on the 25th of that month along with sixty alleged co-conspirators.

Mandelstam, who was closest politically to the Socialist Revolutionaries, spent the years 1917–22 shuttling between Red, White and neutral territory, turning up in Petrograd, Moscow, Crimea, Kiev and Tiflis. His poems reflect not only his own conflicted feelings about Russia's radical transformation but also the confusion in the air. He and Akhmatova, who stayed in Petrograd and wrote mostly personal verse in those years, have one attitude in common: both cast their lots with Russia and its people, regardless of how they feel about the Bolsheviks and their stewardship.

Akhmatova's and Mandelstam's fates during the Soviet era are well known, even legendary. Mandelstam's life ended in tragedy, a death in a transit camp near Vladivostok on 27 December 1938. Akhmatova survived years of persecution under Stalin, which included the long imprisonment of her son Lev Gumilyov. Despite the authorities' best efforts, her death on 5 March 1966 triggered an enormous public outpouring of grief. Her funeral and the memorial services that followed allowed her admirers to mourn her passing, but also to celebrate her personal triumph and her generation's achievement.

Boris Pasternak is known in the West primarily as the author of *Doctor Zhivago* (1957), but he was, first and foremost, a poet. Despite being nominally associated with the Futurist group "Centrifuge" throughout the 1910s, he was personally close to Tsvetaeva, Akhmatova and Mandelstam, while his poetics were all his own. The year 1917 was an enormously stimulating and productive time for the poet, and it was the political turmoil of those days and months that—however indirectly—inspired his first masterpiece, the collection *My Sister, Life*, as well as its companion volume, *Themes and Variations*. 'Spring Rain' is one of only two poems in *My Sister, Life* that makes direct mention of political events, but the whole collection resonates with revolutionary energy. In an autobiographical sketch titled 'People and Propositions', written in 1956–57 but not published until 1967, Pasternak described his and his nation's state between February and October 1917:

A multitude of excited, keenly watchful souls would stop one another, flock together, form crowds and think aloud "in council", as they would have said in the old days [...]. The infectious universality of their elation blurred the boundaries between man and nature. In that famous summer of 1917, in the interval between two revolutionary periods, it seemed that the roads, the trees and the stars were rallying and speechifying right along with the people. The air was seized from end to end with fervid inspiration that blazed for thousands of *versts*—it appeared to be a person with a name, to be clairvoyant and possessed of a soul.

OSIP MANDELSTAM (1891–1938)

Let's praise, O brothers, liberty's dim light,
   the great and sombre year!
   A forest of thick snares is plunged
   into the boiling waters of the night.
   You are ascending into god-forsaken years,
   O people—sun and judge.

   Let's praise the fateful burden
the people's leader shoulders through his tears.
   Let us praise power's sombre burden,
   a weight one can't withstand.
Whoever has a heart, O time, must hear
   your ship sink and descend.

We have bound swallows
   into warring legions—now
   we cannot see the sun; the elements
   all chirp, stir, terribly alive;
   through the thick twilight of the nets
we cannot see the sun, while the Earth sails.

Well then, let's try it: an enormous, ponderous,
   creaking rudder-turn.
   The Earth sails. Courage, men.
   Cleaving the sea as with a plough
   we shall recall, even in Lethe's bitter cold,
that the Earth's price was all ten spheres of paradise.

MAY 1918, MOSCOW
(Translated by Boris Dralyuk)

ANNA AKHMATOVA (1889–1966)

When the nation, suicidal,
awaited German guests,
and Orthodoxy's stringent spirit
departed from the Russian Church,

when Peter's city, once so grand,
knew not who took her,
but passed—a drunken harlot—
hand to hand,

I heard a voice. It called me.
"Come here," it spoke consolingly,
"and leave your senseless, sinful land,
abandon Russia for all time.
I'll scrub your hands free of the blood,
I'll take away your bitter shame,
I'll soothe the pain of loss
and insults with a brand new name."

But cool and calm, I stopped my ears,
refused to hear it,
not letting that unworthy speech
defile my grieving spirit.

AUTUMN 1917

(Translated by Margo Shohl Rosen and Boris Dralyuk)

BORIS PASTERNAK (1890–1960)

Spring Rain

It grinned to the bird-cherry, sobbed and soaked
the gloss of carriages, the flutter of pines.
Under the bulging moon, fiddlers in single file
make their way to the theatre. Citizens, form lines!

Puddles on stone. Like a throat full of tears,
deep in the heart of a rose's furnace
damp diamonds burn, and on them, on clouds,
on eyelids, the wet lash of happiness.

The moon for the first time models in plaster
epic queues, tossing dresses, the power
of enraptured lips; it models a bust
modelled by no one until this hour.

Whose is the heart in which all this blood
rushed from the cheeks, rushed in a flood
to glory? The minister's fingertips
have squeezed together aortas and lips.

Not the night, not the rain, not the chorus
shouting, "Hurrah, Kerensky!" but now
the blinding emergence into the forum
from catacombs thought to have no way out.

Not roses, not mouths, not the roar
of crowds, but here, in the forum, is felt
the surf of Europe's wavering night,
proud of itself on our asphalt.

1917

(Translated by Jon Stallworthy and Peter France)

WAKE ME TOMORROW

E motionally fatigued by the nation's senseless losses in the First
World War and utterly disenchanted with the moribund tsarist
regime, many writers and artists from a variety of backgrounds
were ready to accept the revolutionaries' promises of freedom and
justice for all. Revolutionary enthusiasm seized even the most rarefied
aesthetes, like the openly homosexual poet Mikhail Kuzmin, whose
devotion to "beautiful clarity" (the title of one of his essays from
1910) had so inspired the Acmeists. Kuzmin's diary for 1915–17 is
lost, but his biographers, John E. Malmstad and Nikolay Bogomolov,
have managed to reconstruct their subject's reaction to the February
Revolution:

> The testimony of several other sources indicates that Kuzmin
> was as weary of the senseless killing at the front as were most
> Russians, and that he welcomed a revolution that he hoped
> would bring an end to the war. (His constant anxiety about the

draft status of [his companion Yury] Yurkun should also never be ignored in assessing his response to the events of 1917.) The heroic spirit, the holiday atmosphere, and the air of euphoria he saw everywhere, especially on the 'simple faces' of the peasant soldiers crowding the streets, thoroughly seduced him.

Kuzmin chronicles this seduction in the poem 'Russian Revolution'—as direct and "beautifully clear" an expression of his elation and great hopes as any diary entry. Unfortunately, Kuzmin's hopes for a future free from oppression and fear—both as a writer and a member of a sexual minority—were not to be fulfilled. Yurkun was briefly arrested in 1918, in a wave of "Red Terror", and continuously harassed by the police throughout the next two decades. And although Kuzmin himself continued to work as a theatrical composer, critic, editor and translator, his apolitical verse was rejected as non-Soviet; he withdrew into a small circle of friends and admirers, essentially living a life parallel to that of most of his countrymen, as if the Soviet Union simply did not exist. Conditions grew worse after Stalin came to power. In 1931 Yurkun was forced to become a police informant, while 1933 saw the official outlawing of homosexual activity, of which there had previously been no mention in the Soviet Russian criminal code. Kuzmin died of pneumonia on 1 March 1936, in the midst of the Great Purges, which would engulf many of his close friends, including Yurkun, who was arrested and executed in 1938.

Kuzmin had little time for the work of Sergey Esenin, a poet two decades his junior. Esenin was born into a peasant family in the village of Konstantinovo, near Ryazan. He received a solid education in a church-run school and left home for Moscow in 1912, supporting himself first by working in a butcher's shop, then in a bookshop, then as a typesetter, and attending lectures at the newly opened Shanyavsky People's University. He burst onto the literary scene after moving to

Petrograd in 1915, where he associated himself with the New Peasant poets, growing especially close to their de facto leader, Nikolay Klyuev (1884–1937), who was openly homosexual; this was the first of many intense relationships Esenin—who was thrice married and had many affairs with women—would form with male poets.

Like the other New Peasants, Esenin wrote paeans to a glorified Russian countryside and the rural way of life, combining modernistic technique with folkloric imagery and devices drawn from traditional oral genres. In 1916–17, the peasant poets were championed by a group of intellectuals—the Scythians—who named their movement after a tribe of Iranian nomads that had occupied the area north of the Black Sea between the ninth century BCE and the fourth century CE. To their leading theoretician, Razumnik Ivanov-Razumnik (1878–1946), the spirit of the ancient Scythians—an Asian people on European soil—came to symbolize Russia's special mission in the world: to reconcile the binary opposites of East and West, the rational and the irrational, the natural and the technological, the cultural forces of the common people and those of the intellectuals. With their radical blending of modern and traditional themes and modes, the New Peasant poets represented just such a reconciliation. The Scythians, who were closely associated with what would become the Left faction of the Socialist Revolutionary Party, were essentially romantic anarchists; they believed that a culture remains vital only if it is allowed to develop under conditions of absolute freedom, and they met both the February and October Revolutions with great zeal.

As men of peasant origin, Esenin and Klyuev could be expected to sympathize with revolutionaries who pledged land to the people and an end to the war. After all, in 1916 Esenin had only narrowly avoided being sent into battle—the fate of so many men of his class. Through the intervention of powerful friends, he was stationed at Tsarskoe Selo; he may have been a recognized poet, and had even met the empress, but he was still a peasant soldier—one of those "simple faces" that had won Kuzmin over to the revolutionary cause. Esenin's poem 'Wake me tomorrow at break of day...' was his first poetic reaction to the events of February. Its vibrant imagery both is typical of New Peasant poetry and foreshadows the next step in Esenin's literary career: his joining a movement called Imaginism, with a new close friend, the poet Anatoly Mariengof (1897–1962). Esenin's ecstatic, apocalyptic poems of 1918 demonstrate a deep commitment to the Bolsheviks, drawing on Biblical and folkloric images of transfiguration and salvation.

Yet this commitment was always more emotional than ideological, and by the early 1920s it began to waver. A letter to his friend and fellow Imaginist Alexander Kusikov, written on 7 February 1923 from the deck of a ship on which Esenin was returning to Europe from the United States, testifies to the depth of his disenchantment: "I am ceasing to understand what revolution I belonged to. I can see only one thing—that it was neither the February nor the October, evidently. In us there was and is concealed a kind of November." In his later work, Esenin mourns the demise of the Russian countryside, which had been ravaged by the Civil War and by early Soviet policy, and chronicles his own debauched lifestyle in Moscow's taverns. The self-proclaimed "hooligan" became an idol for young nonconformists and a target of vicious attacks in the official press. He was found hanged in a Leningrad hotel room on 28 December 1925. Although he left a suicide note—a poem written in his own blood—many believe he was killed by the Cheka (the first incarnation of the Soviet secret police).

MIKHAIL KUZMIN (1872–1936)

Russian Revolution

It seems a century has passed, or just one week!
What week? A single day!
Saturn himself was shocked: his scythe
had never spun so quick.
A day before, people were huddled in a gloomy crowd,
jumping aside from time to time and shouting vaguely,
while the Anìchkov Palace fired volley after volley
over its traitorous shoulder in a red and vacant cloud.
News (so routine!) crawled by like snakes:
"Fifty... Two hundred killed..." Cossacks advance.
"They will not shoot!... Refuse..."
The governmental snitches hiss, their collars raised.
Today... Today the rising sun
saw all the gates swung open in the barracks.
No sentinels, policemen, pickets,
as if there never had been any guards or guns.
There's music playing. Fighting's broken out,
but, somehow—not the faintest hint of fear.
The troops have chosen freedom! God—my God!
Everyone's ready to embrace each other.
Remember this—this morning, after that black night—
this sun, this polished brass.
Remember what you never dreamt would come to pass
but what had always burnt within your heart!
The news is ever gayer, like a flock of doves...
"The fortress has been taken! The Admiralty's ours..."
The sky is clearer, bluer up above,
as if Easter had already taken up its post.

Then, towards evening, the owls up in the attics
begin exchanging shots—
seized by blind madness, they are ready
to suffer out their mercenary lives.
Lorries rumble through the streets—
boys driving ministers to the Duma—
a "Hurrah" clings like a cloud of dust
to the motorized clamour.
Laughter? What's the point in being dour?
This is no funeral—we're building a new house.
Will there be space for all of us?
We'll think of that later.
Remember the first dispatches from the Soviets,
the dizzying, "For all, for all, for all!"
It's like telling a starving man, "Eat!"
And him replying, "I'm eating!" with a smile.
Tough sandpaper has polished all our words.
(Renovators of language—and how!)
It seems the word "citizen" is heard
for the first time—invented just now!
The Russian Revolution is youthful, chaste and good—
it doesn't repeat the French, only sees it as an equal,
and it struts down the pavement, plain and simple,
like an angel in a workman's smock.

1917

(Translated by Boris Dralyuk)

SERGEY ESENIN (1895–1925)

Wake me tomorrow at break of day,
my patient mother: that is best.
Then past the mound I'll take my way
and meet at last our longed-for guest.

Today the forest tracks I've traced
where wide-set wheels had cut the mould.
The wind, beneath cloud-groves, had chased
and tweaked his troika-arch of gold.

At dawn he'll rise and rush, he'll dip
his mooncap under bush and tree;
and on the plain his mare will sweep,
waving a red tail in her glee.

Then wake me at the break of day.
Light in our room the lamp, and call.
For soon now I'll become, they say,
a Russian poet known to all.

Our stove, our rooster and roof I'll sing:
you and our guest with songs I'll rouse—
and on my words, on everything,
I'll spill the milk of your red cows.

1917
(Translated by Jack Lindsay)

IRON FLOWERS

No group of writers greeted the victory of the "Workers' Revolution" in October with greater enthusiasm than those who belonged to the victorious working class. The roots of the movement known as Proletkult, or "proletarian culture", date back to the first Russian Revolution. Disillusioned by the failure of the largely intelligentsia-led uprising of 1905, an influential faction of Bolsheviks—including Gorky, the philosopher Alexander Bogdanov (1873–1928) and the future Soviet Commissar of Public Enlightenment Anatoly Lunacharsky (1875–1933)—decided that the party must foster political activism among the proletariat itself. The best way to do this, they theorized, was to cultivate a distinct proletarian culture, which would awaken the workers' class-consciousness by inspiring a sense of independence and pride. Official Proletkult organizations sprang up in Petrograd and Moscow in 1917 and early 1918; soon, with governmental support, the group went national.

One might assume that a "dictatorship of the proletariat" would readily embrace the products of the Proletkult as its official culture—in Marxist terms, as the only appropriate "superstructure" determined by the society's new "base". But almost from the start, the representatives of Proletkult would come into conflict with the Bolshevik regime, which refused to anoint their work as the only acceptable cultural product of the emerging Soviet state; that would mean rejecting and suppressing the work of the Futurists, of the "Fellow Travellers" and of other friendly artists of bourgeois origin, when the Bolsheviks could use as many friends as they could get. Writing in 1924, Leon Trotsky (1879–1940), one of the most discerning readers among the Bolsheviks and an opponent of Proletkult artistic primacy, outlined his—and, to all intents and purposes, the party's—position in the 1920s:

> Every ruling class creates its own culture, and consequently, its own art. History has known the slave-owning cultures of the East and of classic antiquity, the feudal Culture of mediaeval Europe and the bourgeois culture which now rules the world. It would follow from this, that the proletariat has also to create its own culture and its own art.
>
> The question, however, is not as simple as it seems at first glance. [...] Bourgeois culture, if one were to count only from the time of its open and turbulent manifestation, that is, from the period of the Renaissance, has existed five centuries, but it did not reach its greatest flowering until the Nineteenth Century, or, more correctly, the second half of it. History shows that the formation of a new culture which centers around a ruling class demands considerable time and reaches completion only at the period preceding the political decadence of that class.

The proletarian writers, who were, by and large, rigidly orthodox Marxists, perceived the regime's pragmatism as hypocrisy, even downright heresy. The Bolsheviks, for their part, tried to contain and control the organization, subordinating it to the People's Commissariat of Education in 1920. This led to bitter resentment, internal disputes and the formation of splinter groups like Kuznitsa ("The Smithy"), which retained its autonomy and often took a hostile stance towards the Bolsheviks. The government's adoption of the New Economic Policy (NEP) at the end of the Civil War in 1921, a reintroduction of limited capitalism that Lenin famously characterized as "a step backward in order to take two steps forward", proved to be the final disenchantment for many proletarian writers. Two of the poets below, Mikhail Gerasimov and Vladimir Kirillov, resigned from the party in protest. In a self-flagellating lyric of 1923, in which he addresses himself to a "judge", Kirillov goes so far as to reject all his ecstatic writing of the 1910s as a "crime", nothing more than "empty compositions, / all full of dreams, of dreams and lies". In 1937, both Gerasimov and Kirillov were arrested and executed.

Gerasimov was more talented than Kirillov, but both their works resonate with the hope and gargantuan energy of the workers' movement in the revolutionary period. They also show the influence of their "bourgeois" reading. Indeed, formally speaking, the Proletkult poets were quite conservative, employing traditional metres and stanzaic structures. And though Kirillov vows—famously and foolishly—to "burn up Raphael" in order to make room for a new culture, even this threat is, ironically enough, derivative of the Futurists' promise to "toss Pushkin, Dostoevsky, Tolstoy, and so on, and so on, from the steamship of modernity", which they made all the way back in 1912. Gerasimov's rude motors, too, rumble right out of the garage of Futurist poetics, and one cannot help but feel that the poet remains a Symbolist at heart. What are his "iron flowers" but a symbol—a most fitting symbol—for the proletarians' vision of a "tender" pastoral world transformed in their own steely, industrial image? Proletkult's naive "cosmism", with its "iron messiahs" (the title of another Kirillov poem) freeing and refashioning the world, was roundly derided by contemporary poets and critics outside the movement, but it speaks to the promise the October Revolution held for the true believers, and true romantics, of the working class. Alexey Kraysky's 'Decrees' captures this sense of promise even more directly.

MIKHAIL GERASIMOV (1889–1937)

I forged my iron flowers
beneath a workshop's smoky dome—
not amid nature's tender bowers,
or beauty in full bloom.

They weren't caressed by Southern sunshine,
or cradled by the moon—
my thunderous bouquet was burnished
in a forge's fiery storm.

Where motors rumble, rude and awful,
where sirens whistle, metal rings,
I was entranced, I fell in love with
the chime of copper pines.

This workshop dance was tiring,
my palms were hard as rocks—
but a never-tiring fire
blazed in my chest, beneath my smock.

Fed by the dream of Communism,
I stoked the furnace with new power,
intoxicated by its rhythm,
I forged my iron flowers.

1917

(Translated by Boris Dralyuk)

VLADIMIR KIRILLOV (1890–1937)

We

We're Labour's countless, awe-inspiring legions.
We are the conquerors of seas, of oceans and of land.
We've lit the city with the light of artificial suns,
our proud souls blazing with rebellion.

We're seized by mutinous and zealous drunkenness.
Let them decry: "You're beauty's executioners!"
We'll burn up Raphael for our Tomorrow's sake,
trample art's flowers and destroy museums.

We've cast off the oppressive burden of tradition,
rejected the chimeras of its bloodless wisdom.
Venus de Milo cannot match the vision
of young girls in our Future's shining kingdom.

Our eyes have dried, all tenderness is dead—
we can't recall the smell of grass or of spring flowers.
We've fallen for the song of sirens, wheels and shafts,
the might of steam and dynamite's explosive power...

Oh, poet-aesthetes, curse us—the Great Brute you fear!
Kneel, kiss the splinters of the past beneath our feet,
and wash the ruins of the shattered temple with your tears.
We breathe another beauty—we are brave and free!

The muscles of our hands crave labour on a giant scale,
and our collective chest burns with creation's torment.
We'll fill our combs with honey till they spill,
and find a new, dazzling direction for our planet.

We love life, with its heady and exuberant delight.
Our spirit's tempered by a battle fierce and raw.
We're all and everywhere—the flame of victory, its light.
We're our own Deity and Judge and Law.

1917

(Translated by Boris Dralyuk)

ALEXEY KRAYSKY (1891–1941)

Decrees

Through mud, over puddles, she gambols,
selling newspapers—silly young lass.
Her voice is as bright as a sparrow's:
"Decrees! Decrees! Decrees!"

First: "All Power Goes to the Soviets!"
Next: "Peace to All the World!"
The *grandes dames* just cannot get over it—
her cries rattle their nerves.

The generals' epaulettes quiver.
Out of fear? Laughter? Who knows?
The dandies snort, "They'll never
last, these Soviet dogs."

The lass doesn't care—hawks her papers
left and right... Wait, don't you see?
Silly girl, read them and realize:
these decrees are for you and for me.

Dad's at war, choking on gas.
Mum works in consumptive fumes.
They hear your indifferent phrase
and rush to read the news.

They imagine their daughter a commissar
in a land where workers live free...
Silly girl, don't you realize?
These decrees are for you and for me.

1917

(Translated by Boris Dralyuk)

PURIFYING FIRE

In his 1921 obituary of Alexander Blok, the leading light of Russian Symbolism and the dominant poetic figure of the first decade of the twentieth century, the Futurist Vladimir Mayakovsky, whom Stalin would anoint as "the best, the most talented poet of our Soviet era", recalled an incident from "the first days of the Revolution":

> I remember walking past the gaunt, hunched figure of a soldier warming himself at a bonfire in front of the Winter Palace. He hailed me. It was Blok. We walked as far as the Detsky Entrance. "D'you like it?" I asked. "It's good," said Blok, and then added, "They've burned down my library in the country." [...] The Symbolist had to decide which of the two feelings was stronger in him. To praise the "good" or to lament the embers of the fire. Blok never made that choice in his poetry.

Mayakovsky was a sensitive and appreciative reader of Blok, but he seems to have underestimated the degree to which the older poet had anticipated—indeed, had welcomed—the fire that took his library. Like most of his fellow Symbolists, Blok embraced an eschatological vision, fully expecting the dreary, rationalistic, thoroughly corrupt world he had come to detest to be swept away by a destructive, "purifying" fire, which would then give rise to a new, harmonious way of life.

Russian Symbolism, which flourished between 1892 and 1910, was too broad and varied a movement to lend itself to a single, coherent definition, and its mercurial and programmatically irrational adherents would likely rebel against any attempt to pigeonhole them too neatly. Nevertheless, it is safe to say that the poets emerging from the movement shared a conviction that a deeper, richer reality lay beyond the visible world, and that creative artists had a special capacity to access this reality through their extraordinary powers of intuition and observation. Although Symbolism reached a crisis point in 1910, riven by internal disputes and challenged by nascent Acmeism and a variety of Futurisms, the movement's most important poets— especially Blok and his friend and rival Andrey Bely—continued to exert a tremendous influence on succeeding generations. They also continued to look for signs of that deeper reality everywhere, in all manner of relevant and irrelevant manifestations, observing a world on the verge of transformation and renewal, perhaps even hoping to hasten that transformation.

As the poems of Zinaida Gippius demonstrate, the Symbolist mystics differed in their ideas of what the new world would look like, but they felt strongly that the old world had to go—if not go up in flames. For Bely and Blok, the February Revolution announced the coming conflagration; they hailed the October Revolution as its arrival.

In his article 'Intelligentsia and the Revolution', written in January 1918, Blok urged his fellow intellectuals to listen to the music of the revolution with "every cell of your body, with every beat of your heart, with every stirring of your conscience". His great poem *The Twelve*, written that same month, is nothing short of a whole-body response to that music, in all its sublime, discordant splendour: the howl of the wind, the consternation of the bourgeoisie, the drunken solicitations of prostitutes and, above all, the crude songs, snapped-off commands and crackling rifle shots of the Red Guardsmen, clearing out the remnants of the old order with a grand anarchic sweep.

According to most Bolshevik ideologues, of course, Blok had misheard. *The Twelve* was too ambiguous. Was the poet decrying or revelling in the chaos of the revolution? Either way, he had misunderstood its purpose, and he was certainly wrong in placing Christ at the head of the Red Guard regiment. And yet no one could deny the poem's power. Writing in 1924, Trotsky concluded his assessment with a prediction: "To be sure, Blok is not one of ours, but he reached towards us. And in doing so, he broke down. But the result of his impulse is the most significant work of our epoch. His poem, *The Twelve*, will remain for ever." Blok, for his part, stood behind his vision: the revolution *had* filled the air with its music, and he had caught its strains. But the new world that emerged looked nothing like what he had predicted. He found Soviet bureaucracy more oppressive than that of the tsarist regime, and in 1919 he was even briefly arrested on suspicion of plotting against the state. No longer attuned to the sounds around him, he fell silent, passing away on 7 August 1921. The mystical Bely, too, was never quite at home in Soviet Russia, to which he returned from Germany in 1923; growing increasingly eccentric and unstable, he died on 8 January 1934. Legend had it that the cause was sunstroke, but it was likely a cerebral haemorrhage.

ANDREY BELY (1880–1934)

Russia

Blaze, fiery element,
in pillars of thundering fire:
O Russia, Russia, Russia,
rage till I burn with fire.

Into your fateful havocs,
into your depths forlorn,
wing-handed spirits pour
dreams as bright as the morn.

Weep not: O bend your knees
towards the fiery blaze,
the thunder of seraph songs,
the streams of cosmic days.

The rays of His speechless gaze
will warm, when Christ appears,
the arid wastes of shame,
the seas of endless tears.

Though in the sky there is silver
of Saturn and Milky Ways:
seethe, fiery ball of the earth,
with luminous stormy rays.

And you, element of thunder,
rage till I burn away:
O Russia, Russia, Russia,
messiah of the coming day.

AUGUST 1917, POVOROVKA
(Translated by Gerard Shelley)

ALEXANDER BLOK (1880–1921)

The Twelve

I

Black night.
White snow.
Wind, wind!
Knocks you down to the ground.
Wind, wind—
the blessèd world round!

White snow billows
in the wind.
Solid ice beneath the snow.
Slippery—the going's rough—
everyone out on the street
slips—ah!—poor thing!

A rope hangs
from house to house.
On the rope—a banner swings:
"All power to the Constituent Assembly!"
An old woman weeps and keens—
what on earth can this mean?
Who needs such a thing?
Such a big piece of cloth...
When our boys don't have enough
footwraps—naked and unshod...

The old woman, like a hen,
clambers up a snowy hill.
"Holy Mother up in heaven!"
"The Bolsheviks will kill us all!"

Lashing wind!
Dogged frost!
At the crossroads, a bourgeois
lifts his collar, hides his nose.

Who's that there?—Long hair,
a low voice:
"Traitors!
Russia is finished!"
Must be a writer—
a rhetorician…

And over there, his cassock trailing,
sidling behind snowdrifts…
No, these days you're not so jolly,
are you, Comrade Priest?

Remember how you used to strut,
belly poking out—
cross gleaming from that belly
at the gaping crowd?…

A lady wearing astrakhan
turns to her friend:
"We cried such bitter tears…"
she says, then slips—
and down she goes!

Oh, help!
Pull me up!

The wind is gleeful,
happy, mad,
crumples hems,
lays folks flat,
rumples, twists the trembling
monstrous banner:
"All power to the Constituent Assembly"...
and whips words through the air:

... Had an assembly of our own...
... There, in that house...
... Discussed and discussed—
and resolved it, all right:
ten roubles an hour, twenty-five for the night...
... We don't come cheap...
... Now let's catch some sleep...

Getting late.
Empty street.
Only vagrants crouching,
swaying, stumbling,
and the wind whistling...

Hey, poor devil!
Come close—
give us a kiss...

Bread!
What's ahead?
Move along, hurry!

Black, black sky.

Fury, sorrowful fury
seething in the heart...
Black fury, holy fury...

Comrade!
Eyes front!

2

The wind struts, the snow flits.
Twelve men marching through the streets.

Rifle slings as black as night,
fires, fires on all sides.

Fags in their teeth and flattened caps—
should have diamonds on their backs!

Ah, freedom, freedom,
free of the cross!

Tra-ta-ta!

It's cold, Comrade, cold!

"Katya's out with Vanya, drinking..."
"Kerensky roubles in her stocking..."

"And Vanya's rolling in the dough..."
"Our Vanya's in the army now!"

"Well, Vanya, bourgeois cur,
just you try and kiss my girl!"

Ah, freedom, freedom,
free of the cross!
Katya's busy with her Vanya—
what'ya busy at, my lass?…

Tra-ta-ta!

Fires, fires on all sides…
Round their shoulders—rifle slings…

Keep in revolutionary step!
The tireless enemy never sleeps!
Steady, Comrade—you're no sissy!
Take a shot at Holy Russia—

old-fashioned,
hut-dwelling,
fat-assed Russia!

Ah, yes, free of the cross!

3

All our boys, they went to serve—
serve in the Red Guard,
serve in the Red Guard,
lay down their reckless heads!

Oh, you bitter, bitter grief—
oh, you sweet, sweet life!
A ragged coat to keep us warm,
and an Austrian rifle.

We'll give grief to all bourgeois,
set the world on fire—
fire, soaked in blood—
give us Your blessing, Lord!

4

The snow whirls, the coachman snarls,
Vanya and Katya race through the night—
the sled's shafts gleam
in the 'lectric light…
Oh, oh, on they go!…

A soldier's coat on Vanya's back,
a dumb grin on his mug,
whiskers of the blackest black—
he twirls and twirls 'em,
cracks his jokes…

Yes, Vanya—big and strong!
Yes, Vanya—silver-tongued!
Cuddles Katya, silly girl,
casts his slippery spell…

She tosses back her head and smiles,
teeth glimmering like pearls…
Oh, Katya, my Katya—
that fat little face…

That scar the knife left on your neck—
Katya, it ain't healed.
That little cut beneath your breast—
lass, it's bleeding still!

Oh, oh, dance and dance!
Pretty legs—give us a glance!

You wore lacy underwear—
go on, wear it, wear it out!
Played the slut with officers—
go on, go on, play the slut!

Oh, oh, play the slut!
Makes your heart skip a beat!

But that officer of yours—
well, my knife, it never fails…
Don't you remember that, you whore?
Has your memory gone stale?

Oh, oh, freshen it—
take that memory to bed!

Wore grey stockings on your legs,
gobbled "Mignon" chocolates,
used to go out with cadets—
now you're out with soldier boys?

Oh, oh, sin away!
Make your soul feel gay!

6

... Heading for us at full speed—
driver flies and yowls and screams...

Stop! Andrey, give me a hand!
Petrukha, get them from behind!...

Crack-crack-crack! Bullets fly!
Snow dust rising to the sky!...

Driver and Vanya make a run...
One more time! Cock your guns!...

Crack-crack-crack! You'll think twice—
....
before courtin' someone's lass!...

Got away, the dirty rat!
You just wait—I'll get you yet!

Where's that Katya?—Dead, dead!
Took a bullet to the head!

Happy, Katya?—Not a sound...
Lie there, carrion, on the ground!...

Keep in revolutionary step!
The tireless enemy never sleeps!

And again, the twelve march onward,
rifles slung behind their backs.
Only the poor murderer
doesn't show his mug…

He walks on ahead,
picking up his stride.
Scarf wound tight around his neck—
Katya weighing on his mind…

"Why so glum, there, Comrade?"
"Why so quiet, pal?"
"Why so low, Petrukha—
sorry for the girl?"

"Oh, my comrades, my dear friends,
how I loved that lass…
I spent dark and drunken evenings
in her sweet embrace…

"For the devilish daring
in her fiery eyes,
for the crimson birthmark
on her shoulder blade,
I killed her like a dolt—
killed her in a fit!"

"Look, the bastard's wailing—shame!
Petya, what're you, a dame?"
"Wanna bare your soul?
Damn that stuff to hell!"
"Come on, straighten up!"
"Get a goddamn grip!"

"Now just ain't the time
for us to nurse your wounds!
Rougher times will come,
Comrade—and come soon!"

And Petrukha eases up,
slows his pace a bit...

He tosses back his head,
his cheerful self again...

Hey, hey!
Fun's no sin!

Lock your doors, shut 'em tight—
they'll be looting through the night!

Open up the cellars—
treat the thirsty fellas!

8

Oh, you bitter, bitter grief!
Boring, boring boredom—
deadly!

Yes, I guess
I'll bide my time, bide my time...

Yes, I guess
I'll scratch my head, scratch my head...

Yes, I guess
I'll shuck some seeds, shuck some seeds...

And my knife—
yes, I'll slash, how I'll slash!…

Better fly, bourgeois, like a sparrow!
For my sweetie,
for my black-browed beauty,
I'll drink up your blood…
Grant rest to the soul of Thy handmaiden, Lord…

What a bore!

9

The city's silent, not a sound
above the Nevsky tower—
there's no police around—
roam without wine, my brothers!

A bourgeois's standing at the crossroads,
nose buried in his collar.
And near him, tail between its legs,
a mangy mongrel cowers.

The bourgeois stands, a hungry cur,
a question mark, a question begged,
behind him crouches the old world—
a mongrel, tail between its legs.

10

The blizzard's really playing tricks—
playing merry, gay!
Can't see each other, it's so thick,
just four steps away!

The snow circles in a funnel,
rises in a column...

"What a snowstorm—Lord, help!"
"Petya! Cut the crap!
Has the golden icon screen
ever saved you from a thing?
Pal, your head is in the clouds—
think about it, work it out:
Aren't your hands covered in blood
thanks to Katya's love?"
"Keep in revolutionary step!
The tireless foe's around the corner!"

Onward, onward, onward,
working folk!

11

... The twelve go marching on
without the holy name.
They welcome whatever may come,
and don't regret a thing...

They aim their steely rifles
at an unseen foe...
Into blind alleys,
where the wind swirls snow...
At downy snowbanks
that grab your boots and don't let go...

Their red banner
strikes your eyes.

Their measured tread
rings in your ears.

Soon—
their mortal foe will wake.

And the blizzard dusts their eyes,
day and night,
without halt…

Onward, onward,
working folk!

12

… From street to street with sovereign stride…
"Who's there? Don't try to hide!"
But it's only the wind playing
with the red banner ahead.

Cold, cold, cold drifts of snow.
"Who's there? No hiding now!"
But it's only a starving hound
limping along behind.

"Get lost, you mangy cur—
or we'll tickle you with our bayonets.
This is the last of you, old world—
soon we'll smash you to bits."

… The mongrel wolf is baring his fangs—
it's hard to scare him away.
He's drooping his tail, the bastard waif…
"Hey, you there, show your face!"

"Who's that waving our red banner?"
"Wherever I look—it's dark as pitch!"
"Who's that flitting from corner to corner
always out of reach?"

"Best give up, we're warning you—
you won't escape, no matter what!"
"Listen, Comrade, you're all through—
come out or get shot!"

Crack-crack-crack! And the only answer
is echoes, echoes, echoes.
Only the whirlwind's long laughter
criss-crossing the snows.

Crack-crack-crack!
Crack-crack-crack!

… From street to street with sovereign stride,
a hungry cur behind them…
While bearing a blood-stained banner,
blizzard-invisible,
bullet-untouchable,
tenderly treading through snow-swirls,
hung with threads of snow-pearls,
crowned with snowflake roses—
up ahead—is Jesus Christ?

JANUARY 1918

(Translated by Boris Dralyuk and Robert Chandler)

The Scythians

You are but millions. Our unnumbered nations
are as the sands upon the sounding shore.
We are the Scythians! We are the slit-eyed Asians!
Try to wage war with us—you'll try no more!

You've had whole centuries. We—a single hour.
Like serfs obedient to their feudal lord,
we've held the shield between two hostile powers—
old Europe and the barbarous Mongol horde.

Your ancient forge has hammered down the ages,
drowning the distant avalanche's roar.
Messina, Lisbon—these, you thought, were pages
in some strange book of legendary lore.

Full centuries long you've watched our Eastern lands,
fished for our pearls and bartered them for grain;
made mockery of us, while you laid your plans
and oiled your cannon for the great campaign.

The hour has come. Doom wheels on beating wing.
Each day augments the old outrageous score.
Soon not a trace of dead or living thing
shall stand where once your Paestums flowered before.

O ancient world, before your culture dies,
while failing life within you breathes and sinks,
pause and be wise, as Oedipus was wise,
and solve the age-old riddle of the Sphinx.

That Sphinx is Russia. Grieving and exulting,
and weeping black and bloody tears enough,
she stares at you, adoring and insulting,
with love that turns to hate, and hate—to love.

Yes, love! For you of Western lands and birth
no longer know the love our blood enjoys.
You have forgotten there's a love on Earth
that burns like fire and, like all fire, destroys.

We love cold science passionately pursued;
the visionary fire of inspiration;
the salt of Gallic wit, so subtly shrewd,
and the grim genius of the German nation.

We know the hell of a Parisian street,
and Venice, cool in water and in stone;
the scent of lemons in the Southern heat;
the fuming piles of soot-begrimed Cologne.

We love raw flesh, its colour and its stench.
We love to taste it in our hungry maws.
Are we to blame, then, if your ribs should crunch,
fragile between our massive, gentle paws?

We know just how to play the cruel game
of breaking in the most rebellious steeds;
and stubborn captive maids we also tame
and subjugate, to gratify our needs...

Come join us, then! Leave war and war's alarms,
and grasp the hand of peace and amity.
While still there's time, Comrades, lay down your arms!
Let us unite in true fraternity!

But if you spurn us, then we shall not mourn.
We too can reckon perfidy no crime,
and countless generations yet unborn
shall curse your memory till the end of time.

We shall abandon Europe and her charm.
We shall resort to Scythian craft and guile.
Swift to the woods and forests we shall swarm,
and then look back, and smile our slit-eyed smile.

Away to the Urals, all! Quick, leave the land,
and clear the field for trial by blood and sword,
where steel machines that have no soul must stand
and face the fury of the Mongol horde.

But we ourselves, henceforth, we shall not serve
as henchmen holding up the trusty shield.
We'll keep our distance and, slit-eyed, observe
the deadly conflict raging on the field.

We shall not stir, even though the frenzied Huns
plunder the corpses of the slain in battle, drive
their cattle into shrines, burn cities down,
and roast their white-skinned fellow men alive.

O ancient world, arise! For the last time
we call you to the ritual feast and fire
of peace and brotherhood! For the last time,
O hear the summons of the barbarian lyre!

30 JANUARY 1918

(Translated by Alex Miller)

TITSIAN TABIDZE (1895–1937)

Petersburg

Gales from the islands never cease to blow:
They hit the streets that bombs have torched.
The cold is hardest on the flock of sozzled whores.
The freezing ghosts are joined by Edgar Poe.

No clash has ever been so violent.
The greatcoats stink and form a bridal chorus.
The Moyka rinses sailors' bobbing corpses.
The iron Horseman's boisterous heart falls silent.

Who'll hold him back? And who has set him loose?
His acrid sweat has seeped into the marshy ooze.
The only thing they will recall is Lenin's name.

The bloated Dutchman sinks down to the seabed,
While Andrey Bely yelps, a sodden petty demon,
As chaos swallows Petersburg into its phlegm.

1917

(Translated by Donald Rayfield)

OUR MARCH

It's no small irony that Vladimir Mayakovsky, who would sing of the revolution "at the top of his voice" throughout the 1920s, remained all but silent in the first year of Bolshevik rule, producing only a handful of poems. The biggest personality and, along with Velimir Khlebnikov (1885–1922), the greatest talent to emerge from the fervent and fragmented Russian Futurist movement of the 1910s, Mayakovsky was also the Futurist most firmly committed to Marxism. Precocious both artistically and politically, Mayakovsky joined the Bolshevik faction of the Russian Social Democratic Labour Party in 1907, at the age of fourteen. He was arrested three times for "party work"—twice for distributing propaganda, and then on the more serious charge of facilitating the escape of female prisoners. It was while serving an eleven-month sentence in solitary confinement at Moscow's Butyrka prison in 1909 that Mayakovsky decided his contribution to the socialist cause would take a different form. As he recalls in his not altogether reliable autobiography, *I, Myself* (1922, rev.

1928): "I came out in a state of excitement. [...] I wanted to produce a Socialist art. [...] I gave up Party work and sat down to my studies."

In 1911, after enrolling at the Moscow School of Painting, Sculpture and Architecture, Mayakovsky met David Burlyuk (1882–1967), who drew him into his circle of innovative young poets, including Khlebnikov, the poet-aviator Vasily Kamensky (1884–1961) and Alexey Kruchenykh (1886–1968), who pioneered a "transrational" poetics called *zaum*. That same year the "Hylaeans", as they dubbed themselves, would issue a resounding 'Slap in the Face of Public Taste'—a manifesto urging its readers to "Toss Pushkin, Dostoevsky, Tolstoy, and so on, and so on, from the steamship of modernity". Over the next six years, this volatile group—the most artistically diverse and accomplished of myriad factious Futurist outfits—would splinter, then reform as the Cubo-Futurists, then splinter again. Yet despite their internal squabbles, they never lost sight of their true foe: the petty philistine consumer, the repulsive bourgeois. Their aesthetic enemy was, conveniently enough, the class enemy of the Bolsheviks, who were just as single-minded in their hatred. And yet, although the core Hylaeans met the February Revolution with unbridled fervour, the Bolshevik coup induced a more ambiguous reaction.

As Bengt Jangfeldt explains in his magisterial recent biography of Mayakovsky, the poet was disappointed by the Bolsheviks' failure to grant him and his fellow Futurists "priority of interpretation in the discussion of aesthetic matters"; Lunacharsky, the party's leading cultural authority, had instead thrown his support squarely behind Proletkult (see pp. 38–41). Soon, after several rapid shifts in both the Futurists' tactics and the party's policy, Mayakovsky would reconcile himself to Soviet power, but the conflict that surfaced during this period—the conflict between his desire to speak for the workers' state and his need to remain fiercely independent—would never quite resolve itself in his lifetime.

The two political poems that Mayakovsky wrote in the immediate aftermath of October—'An Ode to the Revolution' and 'Our March'—reflect, as Jangfeldt writes, "the general revolutionary frenzy and do not express support for any concrete political line". While 'To Russia', tellingly misdated during the Soviet period to 1915–16 but most likely written in December 1917, speaks, with characteristic tragicomic pathos, to Mayakovsky's romantic vision of himself as an "exotic, outlandish" figure—a tropical ostrich trapped in an "abominable snowland", with little hope of being understood, much less appreciated.

VLADIMIR MAYAKOVSKY (1893–1930)

Our March

Let the squares ring to the tramp of revolt!
Lift your heads' glorious mountain range higher!
We'll cleanse all the cities around the world
with a flood even greater than Noah's.

The days' bull's pied.
The years' cart creaks.
Our god is speed.
Our heart's drum beats.

Is our treasure, our gold not the loftiest thing?
Can we ever be stung by the wasp of a bullet?
Our weapon's the songs that we sing.
Our voices are our gold bullion.

Lay yourself down, grass,
cushion the days' tread.
Rainbow, yoke the years'
galloping steeds' heads.

Look up! The skyful of stars is bored!
We weave our songs without the sky.
Hey, you there! Yes, you, Great Bear!
Demand we be taken to heaven alive.

Drink up the joy! Sing!
The veins' spring's sprung.
Heart! Fight! Ring!
Our breasts are the copper of great kettledrums.

DECEMBER 1917
(Translated by James Womack)

To Russia

Here I come,
an ostrich from a distant land,
wearing these feathers: stanzas, metres, rhymes.
I foolishly try to bury my head,
dig it into my clinking plumes.

I am not yours, abominable snowland.
Soul,
burrow deeper into the down and fluff!
Mine is a different homeland,
I see
a sweltering Southern life.

I'm amid palm trees on a baking island,
perfectly vased.
"Hey,
hit the road!"
They trample on my dreams.
So I go off again
to find a new oasis,
marking my tracks in the sands of time.

At first sight,
some people are unsure of me:
"Should I steer clear of it, does it bite?"
Others stoop to the lowest flattery.
"Mama, hey Mama, does it lay eggs?"
"Beats me, dearest—it shouldn't, but might."

The storeys whinny.
The streets stare.
I'm bathed in the water of frosts.
Riddled with smoke and pointing fingers,
I hurl yet another year into the past.
All right, then, take me in your frozen grip!
Use the wind's razor to cut my feathers.
Exotic, outlandish,
I might as well vanish
under the fury of all Decembers.

DECEMBER 1917

(Translated by James Womack)

PROSE

THE BREAK

Russian authors and intellectuals who witnessed the events of February 1917 in Petrograd—or heard them echo in the provinces or abroad—registered their reactions in verse. Articles celebrating and decrying the collapse of the Romanov dynasty, expressing hope and forecasting the end of days, jostled for column space in the daily newspapers. Fictional treatments of the upheaval, on the other hand, are hard to find. This should come as no surprise: it wasn't so much that the reality of those days was stranger than fiction—it was simply too *real*, too immediate to lend itself to fictionalization. It demanded direct engagement, for which verse and expository prose are usually better suited than even the most veristic of fictional narratives. In the two stories below, the February Revolution intrudes into the authors' fictional worlds in a tellingly oblique manner; in one case it is a sudden rupture, in the other—a melancholy coda.

Alexander Kuprin (1870–1938) was born in the village of Narovchat in the Penza Province of Russia's Volga region. His father, a minor government official, died in 1871, and the family was left without a source of income. His mother, a strong-willed woman who took great pride in her noble Tatar heritage, moved the family to the Widows' Home in Moscow in 1874. The young Kuprin was educated at the Razumovsky boarding school for orphans of the gentry, the Second Moscow Military High School (later renamed the Cadet Corps), and the Alexander Military Academy, from which he graduated with the rank of sub-lieutenant in 1890. Kuprin's experiences at the charitable Razumovsky institution and the two military schools marked him for life; he deplored their intellectually stifling atmosphere, their arbitrary systems of regimentation, and the corporal punishment meted out by sadistic superiors for minor offences. These experiences and attitudes found their way into his fiction, including his excellent novella *The Duel* (1905). Kuprin was an essentially free-spirited man, empathizing deeply with the plight of the downtrodden and drawn irresistibly to a life of adventure. He studied the argot of thieves, wrote about and befriended "French wrestlers" and other circus performers, and was certainly the first Russian author to take off in a rickety Farman biplane (with the famed wrestler Ivan Zaikin [1880–1948] at the helm).

In his characteristically perceptive note on Kuprin in *Contemporary Russian Literature*, D.S. Mirsky makes an invaluable comparison: "He was attracted by Kipling and Jack London (in whose praise he wrote with great eloquence) [...] two or three times he attained something that was not attained by any one of his contemporaries in Russian literature: he wrote several good stories of vigorous and sensational situation with a romantic and heroical keynote." Writing in 1926, Mirsky ends his note definitively: "He is a decided anti-Bolshevik, and emigrated after the fall of the White Army. He is now a resident in France."

That picture, however, is a bit too clean. Kuprin had long harboured anti-monarchist feelings; his early poem 'Dreams' (1887) expressed sympathy for the doomed conspirators who had plotted to assassinate Tsar Alexander III. Three decades later, he greeted the February Revolution with articles celebrating Tsar Nicholas II's abdication and voicing hope for a better future. However, as Nicholas J.L. Luker notes, "Diversity and even confusion characterize his writing [between the revolutions of 1917]. While welcoming the freedom brought by the February Revolution, he foresaw the excesses that further upheaval might bring and feared lest Russia plunge into an orgy of bloodshed." His initial response to the October Revolution was just as ambivalent, and his emigration to France was more a matter of circumstance than principle.

Luker writes, "In the interval between the revolutions of 1917 he published only two new works—the sketch '*Liudi-ptitsy*' (Bird Men) and the tale '*Sashka i Yashka*' (Sasha and Yasha), both of which deal with aviation and contain only a distant reflection of war." In preparing the latter story for publication in France a decade after its composition, Kuprin added a poignant coda—a final paragraph that alters the story's tone as unexpectedly as the events of 1917 altered the course of Russia's history.

The life of an ageing émigré never suited Kuprin, who was, for all his anti-monarchism, a Russian patriot. The collapse of "old Russia" deprived him of the sources of his inspiration, sapped him of his vitality. Impoverished and lonely, Kuprin and his wife returned to the Soviet Union in 1937. His former acquaintances could barely recognize the strapping, vivacious young writer they had once known in the sick old man they now saw before them. Kuprin died of cancer in Moscow on 25 August 1938.

On 12 November 1910, two young boys raced down to the Odessa Hippodrome, a large outdoor venue for sporting events, to witness the wrestler Ivan Zaikin's historic flight in a Farman-16. They were, in fact, "attracted to this flight not so much by Zaikin as by the rumour that Kuprin, the famous writer, who had arrived in Odessa from Petersburg, would be going up with him". The flight was ill-fated: the Farman crash-landed in Odessa's Second Jewish Cemetery. To their fans' relief, both "bird-men" survived:

> The ambulance came trotting jauntily back, empty, followed, at
> a more leisurely pace, by a carriage in which, safe and sound but
> looking a trifle sheepish as they reclined against the cushions,
> rode the Volga Champion, Zaikin, and the eminent writer in his
> Swedish jacket, padded with newspapers to prevent him catching
> cold in the higher atmospheric strata.

One of these boys, and the author of this memoir, would himself go on to become a famous writer—indeed, one of the founders of Soviet literature.

Valentin Kataev (1897–1986) was born in Odessa into an intellectual family. His father taught at a parochial school. He received a partial education at an elite high school (*gymnasium*), where he began writing poems and stories, but left without graduating in order to volunteer for the Imperial Army in 1915, a year after the outbreak of the First World War. He served heroically, was twice wounded and gassed, and was promoted to second lieutenant before being demobilized in 1917. He had published his first stories as early as 1912, but he first received serious attention for his sketches of life at the front.

While convalescing from his wounds in Odessa in 1917 and 1918, Kataev developed a close relationship with other budding Odessan writers, including Yuri Olesha (1899–1960) and the poet Eduard Bagritsky (1895–1934). Along with Isaac Babel (1894–1940), as well as Ilya Ilf (1897–1937) and his writing partner Yevgeny Petrov

(1902–42)—who happened to be Kataev's younger brother—these Odessans would make a major impact on Soviet literature in the 1920s, initiating or contributing to many of its major trends.

Kataev also made the acquaintance of the great Russian author Ivan Bunin (1870–1953), who was fleeing Bolshevik rule in what was then a contested city; starting in December 1918, Odessa was occupied, in turn, by Ukrainian nationalists, Western interventionist forces, the Red Army and the anti-Bolshevik White forces, before finally being retaken by Soviet forces in February 1920. Kataev considered Bunin his teacher, but, in many ways, his temperament is closer to that of Kuprin. He too was an adventurer at heart—a man of action. And the Civil War years were indeed an adventure for Kataev, who may have fought against the Bolsheviks under General Anton Denikin (1872–1947) before going over to the Soviet side in 1920.

This "White" background was thoroughly concealed in the Soviet period, and Kataev showed himself to be utterly faithful to the regime—though not unwilling to intercede on behalf of beleaguered colleagues in times of need, as he reportedly did in the case of Osip Mandelstam (see pp. 25–26). He was also unfailingly supportive of younger authors and, as editor of the journal *Youth* between 1955 and 1966, was an important figure in "the Thaw", the general liberalization of Soviet literature and culture after Stalin's death.

In the 1920s and 1930s, as Soviet literature moved from revolutionary Romanticism and satire to Socialist Realism, Kataev moved with it. His early works responded to the regime's call for a new, ideologically sound literature of adventure, which might attract young readers to the Soviet cause. His highly entertaining novel *The Embezzlers* (1926) satirized the hypertrophied bureaucracy of the NEP era (mid-1920s), when the regime introduced limited capitalism in order to bring the Soviet Union out of a massive economic depression; the policy was then on its way out, so Kataev's attack was, as always, well timed. His *Time, Forward!* (1933), which takes its title from a line by Mayakovsky, is one of the quintessential "novels of construction", depicting an effort by Soviet workers to break a record for pouring concrete in a single day. Kataev's finest work of the 1930s is the poetic *A White Sail Gleams* (1936), which draws on his own childhood in Odessa in depicting the 1905 Revolution from the perspective of two brothers, one eight and the other three years old. All these works are feats of style, as are his late impressionistic autobiographies. At the time of his death from cancer on 12 April 1986, he was regarded as a grand old man of Soviet letters.

His boisterous story 'The Drum', into which the February Revolution bursts like a crash of cymbals, marks the beginning of a glorious career, just as Kuprin's initially boisterous 'Sasha and Yasha' marks a glorious career's eclipse. Reading them back-to-back, one can't help but recall that day at the Odessa Hippodrome, when the young Kataev saw his hero Kuprin falling from the sky.

ALEXANDER KUPRIN (1870–1938)

Sasha and Yasha
An Old Story

Nika the famous fidget. Nika the flea, Nika the nit. Nika, who bounces around like a bucking nanny-goat. Who has to know everything and sticks her pink nose everywhere, especially where it doesn't belong. Give her a minute and she'll give you twenty-five questions and the answers too, before you can so much as think about it.

Nika who isn't even ten yet, but who's flown in a plane twice already and so looks down on her friends from the great height of six hundred metres.

"And it's not the least bit scary," she says. "Just very lovely. It's like riding down the road in a car that doesn't make any noise. And below you everything is laid out like little babies' toys: houses, horses, trains, trees."

Nika comes from a family of fighter pilots, the Prokofievs. Her father's a famous instructor who specializes in heavy combat planes. He dropped bombs on the Germans from a gigantic Farman F30.

Her brother Georgie is known in hangars everywhere as a master of the most difficult acrobatic manoeuvres: no one can match his elegant and perfectly executed loops, slips and spins.

Her other brother, Alexander (Sasha as Nika calls him, simply and impishly) is a maritime fighter pilot. He outranks his father and sometimes, as a joke, offers to help him improve his skills. He's already downed several German planes. He's a senior lieutenant, the handle of his dirk is decorated with a St George's knot, and he'll most certainly get the St George's Cross for his recent performance during the defence of Osel.

Nika's rightfully proud of her three pilots. Even her shabby stuffed monkey Yasha has completed his share of combat missions strapped to the fuselage of Sasha's plane.

Nika scrunches her bright blue eyes, shakes her head like a little boy and brushes away the short hair that has fallen across her nose.

"Look, yesterday you told me about dogs, geese and cats, so today, if you want, I'll tell you about Sasha and Yasha. Only you have to promise not to get mad if I make a mistake."

"Of course, Nika, of course."

Her story is beautiful. It's lively, bright, to the point, and in constant motion. Unfortunately, you'd need a gramophone to get it down, one set up right next to her mouth; though, come to think of it, that wouldn't work either, since over the course of her story Nika whirls around to face every direction. She talks so fast, bubbles appear and pop on her lips. A jumble of words pours from her mouth in a flood, without any order, so that at times it seems like the sixteenth word is reaching you before the fourth.

If you correct her on some sort of technical error, she doesn't care—she's not offended. She willingly admits what she doesn't know, gets right back on track and before you know it has shot off like a skater.

For this reason I'm presenting her story in an abridged form, which I've verified and fleshed out with the help of third parties, occasionally bringing in Nika herself, when her presence is unavoidable.

II

In the middle of the autumn a detachment of military hydroplanes stationed in Osel got a telephone call notifying them that three German submarines had been sighted in the bay of Lou. The news arrived in the early evening, when it was already a little dark. At that moment the only plane on full alert was Sub-Lieutenant Prokofiev's (Nika's Sasha); so, without wasting a second on idle deliberations or unnecessary discussion, the sub-lieutenant hoisted himself into his seat in the hydroplane, along with a gutsy mechanic named Blinov and a pair of half-pood bombs, and, after quickly reaching altitude, set out along the well-known route.

They reached the bay of Lou quickly and without incident; they searched it as thoroughly as possible, but could find no sign of the submarines. After deciding that the trip had been in vain they set off for home, to the great annoyance of Blinov, who was itching to drop the bombs he was holding.

The hydroplane approached its mooring site. The lighthouse at Sorve had already been lit. The flames of the signal fire, which had been deliberately set on the shore, were growing brighter with every second. Tiny black figures could already be seen swarming around it.

Sub-Lieutenant Prokofiev used one hand to steer the plane while the other reached outside the cabin and squeezed the trigger of the electric flash that signalled their return. He managed this with extraordinary deftness, bringing the hydroplane down sharply and settling it onto the water. Blinov went so far as to remark that "even in daylight we couldn't land it that good". Then, suddenly, disaster struck. One of the bombs exploded.

We can only speculate about the cause of the detonation. Most likely it happened as follows: before they had even reached the bay of

Lou, Blinov, seized with impatience, started to pull the safety clip out of one of the bombs. Once he'd removed it completely he hoisted the bomb in his hands, ready to throw it at the first sign (meanwhile, the second bomb lay between his feet at the bottom of the car). When the hydroplane turned around to return home after the unsuccessful search, the mechanic remembered the pin and gripped the bomb between his knees, hoping to put the pin back in place. The bomb was shaped like a pear. It must have slipped and fallen on the other bomb. Incredibly enough, the second bomb wasn't set off by the detonation. The hydroplane was wrecked. Blinov was literally blown to bits. But, by some miracle, the sub-lieutenant was saved.

III

Prokofiev said later that in the moment he didn't hear the explosion and didn't see the burst of flame. All he felt was a kind of demonic strength wrenching him from his seat, tossing him in the air and flinging him into the water. With great effort he scrambled up towards the surface. For a long time the sub-lieutenant was unable to breathe; he kept spitting out the bitter water filling his mouth, throat and nose. Instinctively, he grabbed hold of a broken wing as it floated past him.

He surfaced with his back to the signal fire: a fact that he did not realize immediately. Only five minutes earlier the familiar signals had been burning before his eyes, growing brighter and closer—and now there was nothing except the black, ominous, swelling ocean, the splash of the gloomy waves and utter solitude. And he cried out to the dark, starless sky:

"God! It's horrible!"

He faced the empty shoreless expanse and shouted:

"Help! Help!"

But his strength was abandoning him, his voice was growing weaker and more hoarse. He couldn't understand what had happened to the plane. Had they hit a rock? And where had Blinov gone? And finally, where in God's name were the lighthouse beacon and the signal fire?

Later it struck him that when he tried to feel his right leg with his left foot, he couldn't: it was as if the limb had gone to sleep. But then he accidentally brushed it with his hand. It was floating there, completely disfigured, broken and bobbing around almost at the surface, following the movement of his body as the waves rolled it. And in that second he heard the rushing whirr of an approaching motorboat. For a moment his mind was clear and full of deep joy. Then he passed into a dejected and dreamy numbness.

Prokofiev was barely conscious of what happened next: how they hauled him out of the water and into the boat; how they took him towards the bank; how they applied the initial dressing and then drove him the fifty-three miles to Arensburg in a car loaded to the brim with hay.

He vaguely remembered that somewhere, by lamplight, some doctor had used a pair of scissors to cut off the fragments of exposed bone sticking through the mangled flesh of his toes and asked, "Does that hurt?" And he had answered, through clenched teeth: "No, it doesn't hurt, but hurry up, please hurry up…"

From Arensburg they sent him on a steamship to Tallinn, which is where they sent a telegraph to his father in Petersburg, explaining what had happened.

"Papa was sitting on the couch, with Mama right next to him," Nika says. "Suddenly the telegraph came. Papa opened it, read it, and grabbed his head. He turned to Mama: 'There, read it. His leg is broken in two places. The foot is torn off… We must go to Tallinn.'"

All three of them went.

Nika was allowed to take only one toy with her, her favourite, the one she couldn't part with: a monkey, fluffy, plush, with the kindest face you could ever imagine.

"Maybe he'll cheer Sasha up a little," Nika said as she wrapped the monkey in a blanket.

IV

Sub-Lieutenant Prokofiev wouldn't be cheered so easily. The long, uncomfortable journey, the great loss of blood, the agonizing dressings, the sleeplessness: all this had exhausted and weakened him.

"He was so thin—thin and pale, like a dead person," Nika says in a high, soft voice. "And his lips were whiter than white."

His father couldn't hold back his tears. The sub-lieutenant cried too, whispering in a barely audible voice:

"Am I really never going to fly again?"

Just think: what he mourned then wasn't his fine young life with its charm and great hope—a beautiful life—or the looming horror of a future spent as a cripple. No, what weighed on him like a stone slab was the thought that fate had robbed him of a joy that words cannot describe—the joy of soaring upward, through the clouds, into the clear azure, towards the burning sun, as the triumphant roar of the motor mixed with the proud beating of his heart.

Yes, in those tears flowed the true free spirit of a flying man!

But, strangely enough, the stuffed monkey Yasha really did manage to cheer Prokofiev up and make him smile, after he placed it on his chest and began stroking its soft fur and funny face. A large reserve of life force, sturdy, tenacious and inextinguishable, lay hidden deep inside his battered and bloodless body.

"When we got up to go, Sasha stopped me. 'Please, Nikishka, let the monkey stay with me for tonight. Would that be so hard?'

Naturally this was a difficult thing for me to do, but he asked me so nicely—I just couldn't say no. Then the next day he asked again. And then again and again. He begged me! He says, 'Nika, if you only knew how kind Yasha is to me. At night when I can't sleep and everything hurts he sits next to me and comforts me, telling me to be patient. Let me keep him just one more day.'"

In this way Yasha got used to him and began staying with him all the time—so much so that afterwards he didn't want to go home. He went with Sasha when they changed his bandages and even into the operating room.

They amputated the sub-lieutenant's leg a little below the knee. The doctor couldn't guarantee a successful operation: the patient was terribly weak. But the persistent vitality of his nature saw him through. After the operation, which was performed in Kronstadt, Prokofiev was transported to Petersburg, where, at a field hospital under the command of Admiral Grigorovich, he grew better and better each day, with remarkable speed.

He was completely surprised to find himself recovering next to the best of neighbours: his brother Georgie. A month after the pilots' father had received the telegram from Tallinn, he'd received another from the Gatchina airfield:

"Second Lieutenant George Prokofiev wounded. Both legs broken."

Now father, mother and Nika had two patients to visit.

"Georgie was boring, he kept fussing over his wrapped-up leg," says Nika. "But Sasha was all right. It was like they'd cut off somebody else's leg. He was smiling and singing cheerful songs on his guitar. He wrote them himself, to the tune of 'Margarita':

> Prokofiev doesn't worry 'bout his leg,
> He'll serve his country on a wooden peg...

"Meanwhile Yasha sat on a chair between the two beds, looking very important. So, so important. He didn't even recognize me. One of his legs had been wrapped up too. To keep Sasha and Georgie company."

v

They made Sub-Lieutenant Prokofiev an artificial leg. During the long days while he was getting used to it, all his thought and talk (and probably his dreams and prayers too) were focused on a single worrisome question: Would he or wouldn't he be able to serve his country on a wooden peg? It turned out he would.

Just imagine his uncontrollable joy when, early on a crisp morning in June, he parted from the ground and began floating freely upward, with the aeroplane responding to his fingers' subtle movements the way it always had, keenly and readily, and ruddy Yasha strapped to the fuselage at the nose of the plane, staring haughtily into the sky, with his arms and legs outspread and his head turned defiantly to the side and back, as if to say, "Aren't we something!"

From that point on, Nika's Sasha and the brave monkey Yasha were inseparable. It should be noted that the majority of pilots have their talismans, charms and amulets. French aviators, for example, carry chained silver or gold medallions bearing the image of the prophet Elijah. Others keep a small pouch in their breast pocket, with Psalm 91 sewn into it: "He that dwelleth in the secret place of the Most High…"

Captain Kazakov, who downed sixteen German planes, had an image of St Nicholas mounted on the nose of his cabin. Others refuse to fly without their lucky charms, their stuffed bears, dogs and elephants.

Yasha was dear to Sub-Lieutenant Prokofiev for two reasons: as a lucky charm, and as a reminder of his flying, flitting nanny-goat, his fleet-footed, sharp-eyed, rosy-nosed Nika. Like all fighter pilots he dropped bombs, flew reconnaissance missions and engaged in dog-fights with German planes, and little Yasha, perched on the fuselage, stared death in the face with insolent and defiant cool.

Once the two of them took part in a dogfight that lasted nearly two hours. One of the four downed enemy aeroplanes was defeated by Prokofiev in conjunction with Lieutenant Diterikhs, and was contested. But the glorious victory over another of the planes was his alone. Using a series of tricky manoeuvres, Prokofiev approached the tail of a powerful German "Albatross" and, positioning himself in terrifying proximity, literally rained bullets down on the foe.

The sub-lieutenant saw clearly (and would never forget) as the German pilot fumbled frantically at his machine gun; but the gun had "jammed", as the expression goes, and he was unable to get it working again. The motor of the German plane began to stutter haltingly; the plane listed and began to drop. A fire broke out. Prokofiev watched as the German first clutched his head in despair, and then turned his face, which was red and contorted with rage, towards the Russian pilot, shaking his humungous fists furiously above his head as he rolled his eyes and screamed the most terrible curses. And then both he and his burning aeroplane slipped into a tailspin and plummeted two thousand metres down to the sea.

VI

After he'd docked, Nika's Sasha, whose arm had been lightly wounded, counted the bullet-holes in his plane. Between the shrapnel and the machine guns there seemed to be about thirty holes. Luckily for him, none of the bullets or pieces of shrapnel had hit any of the flying boat's vital areas.

Prokofiev was promoted to lieutenant for that fight, and received the Golden Sword. And Nika says proudly:

"Both my Sasha and my Yasha got their Georges. Sasha's is a white cross on a dagger, and Yasha's is a St George's medallion on his breast. That's how the order said to do it."

"Come now, Nika. That's not really what the order said, is it?"

"Well I can't say for sure. But anyway, they both got their Georges. See for yourself…"

She rummages around in her hope chest and pulls out a hand-tinted photograph. Sure enough, there's the thin, open face of the twenty-two-year-old Lieutenant Prokofiev with his arm tied up in a scarf. And there is Yasha, stuffed, battle-scarred, somewhat surprised, but still cool as ice and with his eyes wide open. His arm is bandaged and there really is a gold-coloured medal made out of cardboard with a striped ribbon pinned to his breast.

"You're right, Nika. My apologies. When Sasha's leg was bandaged, Yasha's leg was bandaged too. The same with their arms. And when machine-gun bullets rained down on Sasha, they rained down on Yasha too. If Sasha has a gold medal now, then why shouldn't Yasha strut around wearing an orange-and-black ribbon?"

That's the end of Nika's story. The only thing left to add is that the one-legged Lieutenant Prokofiev was able to bring down two more German fighters during Operation Albion. He was there when the Germans bombarded Tserelsky with fourteen-inch shells. When he got the order from his superiors to fly with a detachment of fighters to Tallinn, the Tserelsky artillerymen begged him:

"Please stay, Lieutenant. Without you, we're goners."

Prokofiev answered:

"I'm a soldier first and foremost, and follow orders without question. Call them on the radio."

They called and received the following answer:

"Whether or not the lieutenant stays is up to him."

He stayed, and continued to stay until the hangars and two-storey dormitories at the airport had been turned into pitiful piles of rubble under the onslaught of the Germans' monstrous seventy-pood shells. Only then did he order his men to retreat and fly to Tallinn; he himself was last to leave, getting caught in a dogfight during which he was wounded.

The Germans knew him well. Captured pilots spoke his name with respect and could list the names of the planes that he had brought down. And, of course, they all knew about Yasha. Naturally, every one of them had their own good luck charm.

All this came back to me a few days ago, as I looked through old photographs. Some ten or twelve years have passed since that time, but it feels like a hundred, or two hundred. It feels like none of it ever existed: the glorious army, the extraordinary soldiers, the heroic officers, our dear, good, carefree comfortable Russian life… It was all a dream… The old album's pages tremble in my hand as I turn them…

SEPTEMBER 1917

(Translated by Josh Billings)

VALENTIN KATAEV (1897–1986)

The Drum

I

The day after the senior cadets had been made into officers, when a lot of places in the orchestra had opened up, I said:

"Zhuravlyov, pick me for the orchestra."

Cadet Zhuravlyov, the chief orchestra member, who was hale and stocky but looked like a greenhorn, stared at me in surprise and said:

"What's your instrument?"

"The big drum," I lied firmly.

Zhuravlyov knew I wrote poems, an activity that he did not associate with drum-playing. His eyes narrowed sceptically.

"You can play?"

"I can."

Zhuravlyov scratched behind his ear and gave me a searching look. I could not muster sufficient impudence to hold his honest, open gaze and lowered my eyes. Then Zhuravlyov said:

"You can't play the drum, Petrov."

"What's there to play? You take the stick and beat on the, that... The important part for me, you know, isn't the drum, it's the extra hour of leave."

In our academy musicians were granted an extra hour of leave. My argument must have worked, because Zhuravlyov sighed deeply and pulled a notepad out of his pocket and wrote my name on it, and added the word "drum". But later that night as we were sitting across from one another on our bunks and taking off our boots, Zhuravlyov suddenly gave me a frightened look and said:

"Petrov, listen to me, if you only… It's not like your poems…"

I understood that he was referring to the drum, and said:

"Don't worry."

Five minutes later I stuck my head out from underneath the covers. I had a burning question.

"Zhuravlyov, are you asleep?"

"Yes, I'm asleep," Zhuravlyov said in a drowsy, angry voice.

"Listen, will I be able to sign up for that extra hour this Sunday?"

"Yes," Zhuravlyov muttered from beneath his covers, and then no doubt fell immediately asleep.

I thought about the girl on whose account I'd got involved in this whole risky drum business in the first place. Risky, because only once in my entire life had I laid hands on a drum. It happened at a childhood party, when I made my way up to a drum, the kind whose solidity and shine had always captivated me, and gave its taught, translucent, silly face a flick. A soldier with a red moustache said angrily:

"Don't touch."

That day it became clear to me that the career of humble horse-cart driver, of which I had dreamt so passionately as a child, and for which I'd been preparing assiduously since I was three years old, couldn't hold a candle to the glorious and refined work of a drummer. I decided definitively that I'd be a drummer when I grew up, and when little kids tried to touch my drum, I'd snap at them angrily: "Don't touch!"

My childhood dream appeared to be coming true. The next morning Zhuravlyov gave me another searching look and said:

"Don't forget, Petrov—as the drum goes, so goes the rest of the orchestra."

This was news to me. I was ready for anything—anything except that. I had imagined things were simpler: the orchestra took care of itself, and the drummer contributed to the overall success. As inspiration seized him. Nevertheless, I decided to see things through and said to Zhuravlyov:

"I'm tired of all this drum talk. Don't worry. I can play."

At breakfast, Zhuravlyov persisted:

"But maybe you can't play, Petrov. It's better to tell me straight out."

"For god's sake, I can definitely play. I've even been in an orchestra. We had one... at school. And it wasn't bad, either. A perfectly fine orchestra."

"You aren't lying, are you?"

Zhuravlyov was positively fanatical when it came to his work. You should have seen how passionately he wooed cornet-players, bassists and baritones to the orchestra. But all the same, he was annoying me.

If it hadn't been for Zinochka, I would have confessed everything. But a man is capable of all kinds of idiocy for the sake of an extra hour with his beloved. One could write whole treatises on this theme, but that isn't something I'm planning to do here.

II

Up to that point my life had been easy and comparatively worry-free. Mornings I spent in lectures on tactics, fortifications and artillery, dreaming wondrous gilded dreams about officer's breeches and single-starred epaulettes. During after-breakfast drills I inhaled the healthy winter air, and if the company sang songs while it marched through town towards the sea, I sang too, as loudly as I could. My voice was strong and resembled the wail of a dying swan. Moreover, I was essentially tone-deaf. This was why, when I got especially carried away, passers-by stopped and smiled, and my compatriots laughed themselves into such a frenzy that they stopped marching in step. By the time we reached school we were tired and hungry and would head straight for lunch. Then, in the evening, we prepared for parade rehearsal. And later, in bed, a shimmering vision of officers' breeches and gold epaulettes rose before our dreamy eyes. And every night, without fail, someone would announce the good news as they drifted off:

"Gentlemen, let it be known that if you don't count tomorrow, and Sundays, there are fifty days left until graduation."

Now the drum had poisoned my existence. All it took was for me to start daydreaming about something for my conscience to enquire with a malicious hiss: "Didn't you know, Cadet Petrov, that as the drum goes, so goes the rest of the orchestra?" Alas, I did know that, and was suffering. But when it turned out that the orchestra also had a conductor, I fell into a black melancholy, imagining them expelling me from the orchestra after the first practice and revoking my leave for a month.

The next day, before lunch, when all the companies were gathered together in the mess hall, the platoon commander on duty announced:

"Attention! Cadet Krinkin from Second Company has received a telegram. Twenty copecks, a field manual and a handkerchief were found in the tea room. See the platoon commander on duty. After reveille the singers will gather for rehearsal and the musicians for practice." And, having caught sight of the duty officer, he yelled: "Quiet, battalion!"

All through the song, and then as we ate, I toyed with the idea of killing myself. After lunch Zhuravlyov said:

"Don't forget, Petrov—practice is right after lunch."

It was strange: a quiet had settled in my soul, as if before a battle. "Whatever will be, will be," I thought, surprising myself with my coolness.

Death before dishonour. After the aforementioned reveille, I ran determinedly to the third-floor storage room, where they were handing out the instruments. Cadet musicians were already gathering near the storage room, and the stairwell resounded with the quacking of trombones and the snaking warbles of flutes. Next to my drum a thin cadet stood spinning golden cymbals perplexedly in his hand. He was trying to give his face an expression of unconcern—it wasn't his first time playing cymbals just like these, buddy. I went up to the drum, gave it two solid whacks on the side and asked the scrawny cadet:

"Don't you find that they keep this drum a bit loose, Cadet?"

The cadet took a turn tapping his thumb against the drum, and said:

"Maybe a little, but then again…"

I sighed. Him too.

"How long have you been playing the cymbals?"

"Quite a while, actually. In Tiflis I played in the symphony orchestra. The cymbals we had in Tiflis were silver—for the sound."

"Yes, of course—so tell me, how should one play the drum?" I cautiously attempted to sound him out. "I know of course, but I'd like to have your opinion. What I mean is, what did you guys in the Tiflis symphony orchestra do to get the necessary sound?"

"That's easy enough: we used a mallet. Get a mallet, and then hit it like this."

He picked up a mallet and struck it diagonally across the skin a couple of times.

A thick, rubbery sound bounced down the stairs like a soccer ball. The cadet put down the mallet and asked:

"Can't you play?"

"I can play, but I've forgotten a few things. I have to admit, it's been a long time."

Neither of us said anything.

"And when do you hit it? On a count, or some other way?"

"Yes, on a count. When they play a march, the beat is on the left leg—one, two, one, two. But since all we play is marches, the beat is always on the left leg. Same thing with the cymbals, as far as I know."

"And do you think they'll let us take that extra hour this Sunday?"

"I think they will."

I looked at him, he looked at me, and we both broke out laughing. I took my drum with its mallet, he took his cymbals, and we ran down the stairs along with everyone else. We put on our overcoats and caps and crossed the yard to the arena where exercise and practice sessions are usually held. It was dark and cold in the arena. A couple of lamps had been lit. Music stands had been set up. I set the drum up on a saw-horse, and felt a shiver run up my spine. I tried to strike the mallet diagonally, as the thin cadet had done. Zhuravlyov watched me closely; he wanted to say something, but he didn't: he just sighed. The conductor arrived. "Quiet!" Zhuravlyov ordered. The conductor was a short, stocky Czech. He had waddling bow legs, epaulettes on which his bureaucratic rank was proudly displayed, and a pancake hat. There was a large red mole on his cheek, like a plum. He said:

"Hello. How colt and vindy it is. Positively menacing. But ve von't vaste time—it's already late. Let's begin."

He took a moment with each musician, gripping the valves of a trumpet, turning the pages of a score, fussing and saying:

"By Gott, by Gott!"

Finally, he calmed down and said:

"All right, oo-pen march fourteen."

Scores rustled. Copper trumpets glistened. My neighbour waved his cymbals aggressively. The conductor tapped his pencil ominously against the music stand.

"Attention. Tree, four."

He waved his hand and tapped his foot so fervently that it was impossible not to strike the drum with the mallet. And strike it I did. The cymbals crashed, the trumpets roared in various keys, like a herd of elephants. The flute wailed at the wrong moment.

"By Gott, vat are you doing?" The conductor yelled, instinctively covering his musical ears. "For the luff of Gott, stop."

"As you were!" Zhuravlyov yelled. In that moment, he was a giant.

We fell silent in bits and pieces, instead of all at once. The conductor launched himself towards the first person his eyes fell upon. Unfortunately, that happened to be me.

"Vat are you doing? How can you play drum like that? Half you even played drum before?"

"It's all over," I thought, and lied hesitantly:

"I have played, Mr Conductor, sir."

"Vere could you have played?"

"In the… the Fifth Gymnasium. We had our own orchestra there."

"Vat you are telling me is total fairy tale, by Gott. I vas conductor at Fifth Gymnasium for twenty-fife years. Not vonce did I see you."

He stared out at everyone with large angry eyes and suddenly smiled.

"Hee-hee-hee! Vell, so it goes. Ve vill learn. Vun more time. Attention. Two, tree, four."

Everyone laughed. The storm had passed.

This time, it went better. The conductor bawled out one of the bassists—but, my Lord, what a complicated art it was, this drumming! The trumpets roar on all sides, the bass shoots like a bullet into your left ear, the thin cadet's cymbals rumble to your right, while you've got to keep your mind on the *one, two, one, two,* and follow the conductor's hand, which chops fiercely at the groaning air.

The drama of it!

IV

In short, when I showed up at the next practice with my drum, the cadets smiled and someone even shouted:

"Quiet!"

I set the drum on the saw-horse and said:

"Behold: pure art!"

We played marches, and all the while I was thinking that if it was this hard to play on an ordinary Turkish drum in a makeshift cadets' orchestra, where it's all you can do to keep the beat, then how wonderful to be a composer like, say, Scriabin, and to write the *Prometheus,* with its terribly complex score. And I thought too about the fate of all drummers. And my heart cried over their misshapen lives. What could be more stupid than to play the drum? March after march, banging away at its sensitive skin: "One, two, left, left." They play 'God Save the Tsar', and you follow the conductor's gnarled hand and try to keep the beat. Ridiculous!

My love life was going better. On Sunday during leave I signed myself out until midnight and raced over to her at six sharp. Outside was a wonderful, downy winter. The wind scattered the snow. Purple evening lanterns burned along the street.

"Driver!"

The horse trots down the streets, which are unrecognizable under the snow. How I love my little darling! My little black-haired girl with the birthmark over her upper lip. Do I deserve to be so terribly happy?

I'll give the driver a rouble, so that he'll be happy too. Or should I? No, I'll give it to him.

The presence of a woman brings harmony and warmth into a man's life. Actually, that wasn't quite the case here. It wasn't so much harmony as discord. On the one hand there was the perfumed lilac envelope I received every Thursday from the on-duty officer; on the other, the seven I scored in manoeuvres and the two days of "house arrest" I got for not paying attention in formations. Now I was enjoying playing the drum. It didn't matter what we played. I even chose to play through one of my extra hours of leave.

Winter, as a poet might put it, gave way to a misty haze. The wind started blowing from the south, instead of the north. The starlings flew in from somewhere, crowded around the eaves of the houses, and made such a racket that it hurt your head. We were already going to practice without our greatcoats, and when we ran through the puddles across the yard, it was difficult to keep the wind from tearing the drum out of my hands. The wind blew in your face and overcame you entirely; it was cold and glorious. Graduation was nearing and with it that drunk-ecstatic state that always comes whether you're graduating from a regular school or a military one—either way, it's the same thing.

V

And then suddenly something happened, something strange, incomprehensible and unexpected. At first it was merely hinted at, in corners. Then the talk grew louder, at lunch or breakfast. Scraps of rumour, new moods, new words began to leak through the thick, dense walls of the academy, which up to that point had not allowed a single sound or ray of light to penetrate through to us. Something spontaneous and inevitable was brewing in the land. All day we walked around as if lost; we talked and talked, but still couldn't get to the bottom of it. We read newspapers, but learnt nothing concrete. Then came the evening when, in a class on machine-gun use, we listened with tense attention as the captain said something technical about return springs and recoil buffer, something we didn't understand in the least, because we were thinking about something else. In walked cadet Doroshevsky. He was agitated, and didn't even ask permission to come in. He said something to the people sitting on the back benches. A whisper rose up like a wind in a ripe wheat field, and after a minute everyone knew that the tsar had abdicated the throne.

We stopped listening; all we could do was talk. And it seemed that the entire academy was charged like a Leyden jar with intense and fast-moving thoughts. Life burst in on us from the outside, showering us with newspapers, telegrams and rumours. In the evening, the head of the academy gathered us together on the main floor and read two manifestos concerning the abdications of Nicholas and Michael. No one could sleep, we were so worked up. The officers didn't know what to do. That night a telephone call came from somewhere, ordering us to prepare for engagement with guns and live ammunition. The next morning someone from the Fourth Company arrived with a red bow on his chest. There was a lot of noise in our class section. Someone said, sweatily and anxiously:

"Comrades, well, how wonderful this is! Who would have thought, in three days!"

Then word spread that there would be a soldiers' demonstration at twelve o'clock. The truth was, no one from our regiment knew anything, because no one had told us anything about it.

But we were worried.

"Comrades!" came the guttural wheeze of Prince Gardaphadze, an honest and stupid Georgian. "Ammunition must be procured from the master-at-arms. We might have to open fire."

But everyone just laughed at him, which made him upset.

"Those mutton-heads don't understand—we'll have to open fire."

Everything was chaotic and jolly. At fifteen minutes to twelve we were ordered to line up.

At ten to twelve Zhuravlyov ran up to me, cornet in hand, and said, breathing hard:

"Go upstairs. Get the drum. You're going to play. We're going to play."

"Ah, I beg your pardon, but I can't. I don't know how."

"It's swinish not to know how, at a time like this. You have to."

"Give me a gun."

"That'd be swinish too. You're the only one who can do it. Remember, as the drum goes, so goes the orchestra."

I could hear the despair in his voice. "Well, well," I thought smugly.

"Petrov, you will walk at the head of the battalion."

"But how am I supposed to carry it? What will we play? I'll be disgraced. Listen, I'll be practically making it up as I go," I said with despair.

"It won't be the first time!"

I was a dead man. The entire orchestra helped me get the drum on, tightening the belt. They encouraged me. They told me not to despair. They laughed at me. Bit by bit, I worked up some enthusiasm. At the end of the day a drum was no worse than a gun. Even better. True, with a gun you looked manly and fierce. But, on the other hand, as the drum goes, so goes the orchestra—that's how Zhuravlyov put it. And as the orchestra goes—well, so goes the entire battalion. After all, isn't it the orchestra that gets everyone marching in step—isn't it the orchestra that inspires them?

Yes, the orchestra!

VI

The whole academy gathered together on the road in front of the main building. The orchestra was on the right flank. And there I was, with the drum slung across my belly. The head of the academy came out. His greatcoat, with its red lining, was blown open by the wind. He saluted us with these words:

"Greetings, Comrades!"

"The old fox," we thought; but we answered him in unison, as if we were one man. His commands were clear. Rifles clicked. And the battalion made its way down the wet spring street, in a strict column, unit after unit. On the horizon, between the sun-lit houses, a crowd of men ran carrying a red flag. A large freight truck shot past. The bayonets sparkled. We heard music and loud cries, and it was clear that the streets were full of people.

It was all so strange and extraordinary. The pedestrians were all drab-looking, simple people. They stared at us with curiosity and pleasure. And when we flowed into the endless flood of red flags, faces, cars, the sun, the melting snow, the young men, Zhuravlyov's face took on a solemn, ominous expression, and he commanded:

"Let's begin. March fourteen. Only together this time, gentle-men."

He counted off a beat and we struck up. The thin cadet made a magnificent revolutionary. He crashed his cymbals together ecstatically, and always in the wrong place. Blinding shafts of sunlight glinted off the glowing copper of the trumpets, in which the blue sky was cast in green, precisely and hilariously, along with houses, red flags and the faces of the musicians. The street was crammed with agitated people. The soldiers moved forward in an unbroken stream, and we had to wait for the road to clear at practically every crosswalk. It was senseless and glorious. The closer we got to the main square, the drunker we grew with the noise, the more dazzled. Students waved their caps and shouted in hoarse young voices, trying to out-shout one another:

"Long live our comrade cadets!"

We walked down the wet and smelly street where the poor Jews lived, and the dirty, unkempt, lop-eared children swarmed to our orchestra like flies to a sugar cube. The old grey-haired Jews with their *payots* took their hats off, and the pregnant Jewesses laid their hands on their huge bellies and smiled, tears streaming down their cheeks. The company commander was walking in front of me, and the entire time I kept my eyes on his curved and powerful back and his boots covered in dirt. A young Jewess, ruddy and full-breasted, pulled her skirt up to her knees and ran after us, splashing through puddles, until she reached the company commander, caught hold of his overcoat, shrieked, "Oy, you angel!" and tried to give him a kiss. Without changing his step the company commander gave her a frightened look through his pince-nez and waved her away. The cadets smiled, and I saw how the Jewess's eyes blazed with a bright drunken delight. We played the *Marseillaise* over and over again, and I was no longer afraid of messing up, and even occasionally said to the musicians:

"Don't rush. Slower."

The thin cadet beamed, his cymbals glinting. We were all in the clouds.

We made it back to the academy in time for lunch, exhausted by the sun, the air and the crowds. After the sun and the bright colours, the building seemed chilly and dark, and it smelt like uniforms and cabbage soup. Our leadership class was cancelled, and we sat in the classroom talking into the night. We talked about our upcoming graduation, about freedom, about women, about politics; someone even told some off-colour jokes, and everyone laughed. We were full of joy, and our nerves were raw. When I lay down to sleep, Zhuravlyov said:

"You see, Petrov, didn't I tell you that as the drum goes, so goes the orchestra?"

"Gentlemen, I am pleased to inform you that if you don't count Sundays and tomorrow, there are two weeks left until discharge," someone said dreamily.

"Quiet," the orderly said angrily.

I pulled the cover over my head and was unable to close my eyes—so many thoughts and impressions were knocking around inside me. It seemed as if my head was swelling with it all. There was no way I was going to sleep.

"Zhuravlyov, are you sleeping?"

"No. I can't sleep."

"Listen, Zhuravlyov, was I really great today on the drum?"

"You were great. If there was any justice in the world, you'd get two extra hours' leave this Sunday."

"Quiet!" bellowed the orderly.

"What do I need two hours' leave for?" I thought. "Zina?"

But at that minute she was the last thing on my mind.

That night I dreamt some sort of nonsense, a sort of fever-dream, which made my head hurt. The next morning Zhuravlyov pulled on his boots, let out a huge yawn and said:

"You see, Petrov, I told you that as the drum goes, so goes the orchestra. And you didn't believe me."

Then he added:

"Actually, I think I already told you that yesterday."

"If you don't count tomorrow and Sundays, gentlemen, we have two weeks left," someone said.

"Make those beds!" the orderly shouted. "New lieutenant on duty. Lavrishin. First Revolutionary officers. Trumpet-call in five minutes."

AUGUST 1917

(Translated by Josh Billings)

THE RED TRAIN

Limiting the scope of this anthology to works written before 1920 inevitably skews the prose section in an anti-Bolshevik direction. The great prose works of Soviet literature chronicling the revolution and the Civil War from the Reds' perspective—Vsevolod Ivanov's (1895–1963) *Armoured Train 14–69* (1922), Dmitry Furmanov's (1891–1926) *Chapayev* (1923), Isaac Babel's (1894–1940) *Red Cavalry* (1926), and a number of lesser-known but no less stirring novels and stories by the likes of Lidiya Seyfullina (1889–1954), Leonid Leonov (1899–1994), and Alexander Fadeyev (1901–56)—began to emerge in the 1920s, after the Bolsheviks laid down their arms and turned more of their attention to the cultural front. Many early Soviet authors were children of the century, their sensibilities forged in the crucible of 1914–21, a period of uninterrupted strife and privation. In 1921, the poet Nikolay Tikhonov (1896–1979)—who volunteered for the Imperial Army in 1914, joined the Reds in 1918 and was not demobilized until 1922—described his generation's long tempering:

Fire, the rope, the bullet, and the axe—
they bowed to us like servants, followed us,
and torrents slept in every drop of water,
and from each pebble sprang a mountain range,
and every tiny twig crushed underfoot
released the rustling of a black-armed forest.

Lies dined with us and drank with us each night,
bells clanged and clanged simply from force of habit,
coins lost their weight and even lost their ring,
and children weren't frightened of the dead...
Yes, it was then that we first learnt by heart
words that are glorious, bitter, and brutal.

The revolutions of 1917 caught these men and women not only at
the dawn of their literary careers, but at the very dawn of their adult
lives. It took time for them to process their formative experiences and
to shape them into art. But there were older authors who greeted
the events of February and October with open arms—authors who
had witnessed and, in many cases, tasted their share of persecution
under the tsarist regime.

Among the most enthusiastic early supporters of the Bolsheviks
was Alexander Serafimovich (né Popov, 1863–1949), a Don Cossack
who became involved in Marxist revolutionary activity as early as
1883, during his student days at St Petersburg University. There he met
and befriended Lenin's older brother, Alexander Ulyanov (1866–87).
Ulyanov was executed for masterminding a failed plot to assassi-
nate Tsar Alexander III, while Serafimovich, who was implicated in
the affair, was arrested and exiled to the Arkhangelsk Province in
north-western Russia. It was during his exile that he began to write
fiction, winning praise for his sensitive depictions of nature. After his
release from exile, he first returned to his native Don region, then

moved to Moscow in 1902, where he joined Wednesday (*Sreda*), an important literary group whose members included such luminaries as Anton Chekhov, Ivan Bunin and Maxim Gorky.

Serafimovich officially became a Bolshevik in 1918, but he had begun writing for *Izvestia* (News), one of the party's official organs, in the summer of 1917. His fiery, unabashedly propagandistic contributions to that paper, its sister publication *Pravda*, and his own journal, *Tvorchestvo* (Art), over the following two years included dispatches from the front lines of the Civil War, reports on Soviet progress, and harrowing "true stories" of tsarist-era atrocities. 'How He Died' is a powerful example of the last of these categories. Its thrust is clear: those who exploited the weak under the old regime shall now reap what they sowed.

Serafimovich's most famous work is *The Iron Flood* (1924), an intensely lyrical novel of a Red Army unit's arduous escape from White encirclement in 1918; as the title suggests, the work depicts the men as a single, unstoppable, multi-voiced heroic mass. The author became a mentor to a number of budding Soviet writers and exerted a particularly strong influence on Mikhail Sholokhov (1905–84), whose proto-Socialist Realist epic of Cossack life *And Quiet Flows the Don* (1925–40) would win him a permanent place in the Soviet pantheon, as well as the 1965 Nobel Prize in Literature.

Like many progressive authors of the pre-revolutionary period, Serafimovich was moved not only by the plight of Russian peasants and workers, but also by that of the Jews, perhaps the most disadvantaged community in the empire. In 1906, after a wave of devastating pogroms across Ukraine and Bessarabia, Serafimovich wrote a short story, later turned into a play, about a hypocritical bourgeois family that takes in a group of Jews during a pogrom only to surrender them to the mob when their own personal safety is at stake.

At that time Russian Jewish authors were also beginning to speak for themselves—in Russian, Hebrew and, increasingly, in Yiddish. Dovid Bergelson (1884–1952) was born near Uman, in what is now Ukraine, and raised in Warsaw, Kiev and Odessa, the provincial capitals within the restrictive Pale of Jewish Settlement. His first literary efforts were in Hebrew and Russian, but it was in Yiddish that Bergelson was to make his mark, becoming one of its finest modernist stylists. The revolutions of 1917, which promised liberty and equality to Russian Jews, found him in Kiev, where he was involved in the project of establishing Jewish cultural autonomy in Ukraine. As his expressionistic 'Scenes from the Revolution' demonstrates, he reacted to the news with a mix of shock, euphoria and trepidation—for even the joyous round dance of freedom may have something nefarious at its "bellybutton".

Bergelson left Soviet Russia for Kaunas, Lithuania, in 1921, and ended up in Berlin the next year. During his first years in emigration he was highly critical of the Bolshevik regime, but his attitude gradually changed, and by 1926 he had decided that the USSR offered Yiddish culture its best chance to flourish. Bergelson renewed his contacts with Soviet authors and authorities, and eventually returned in 1934. He did his best to conform to the demands of Socialist Realism and, along with many prominent figures in Soviet Yiddish culture, was an active member of the Jewish Anti-Fascist Committee during the Second World War. Many of the committee members were arrested in the winter of 1949; fifteen were subjected to a show trial in 1952, and thirteen—including Bergelson, Perets Markish (1895–1952), Itsik Fefer (1900–52), Dovid Hofshteyn (1889–1952) and Leyb Kvitko (1890 or 1893–1952)—were executed on 12 August of that year, the so-called "Night of the Murdered Poets".

ALEXANDER SERAFIMOVICH (1863–1949)

How He Died
(A True Story)

By a sea of the deepest blue, at the foot of the green Crimean mountains, stretched out the tsar's enormous estate—Livadia.

The estate lacked for nothing. There were fabulous trees and tropical flowers, fine vineyards and fountains, and exotic fruits—the only thing missing was sweet ambrosia.

But inside the white palaces, awash with opulence, a drunken, dissolute life went on: the tsar drank, grand and not so grand dukes drank, barons, counts, priests, generals and officers drank—the whole pack of them crowding around him—and together they ate the Russian people out of house and home. And so that no one should disturb the merry throng, the whole estate was surrounded by barbed-wire fences, and in the barracks were stationed joint companies that guarded the tsar and his gluttonous band day and night. The soldiers were specially selected—each and every one a fine, strapping young man. They were well fed and well kept, but the living was dull and miserable. They kept strict watch, for hours at a stretch they would sit at the listening post, peering through binoculars and telescopes at the highway, at the mountain tracks, at the woods, at the sea—God forbid some suspicious fellow should show up, God forbid someone should make an attempt on the tsar's drunken but nonetheless "holy" personage.

And if a ship or a boat crossed the sea, passing the estate half a mile away, they would shoot to kill.

They were rarely given leave to go into the town of Yalta, which lay nearby, and even when they were, it was never for pleasure: they would go about in detachments, in tight formation, and all eyes—lest they fail to spot an officer. If you took your time saluting, or did it without quite enough youthful zeal, it would mean isolation, bread and water, the disciplinary barracks.

In town they wanted to live a normal human life, like everyone else, calmly and freely, to take even the littlest break from it all, but this too was forbidden; it was forbidden even to speak with those who were at liberty—and then the town, its environs, even the whole of the Crimea swarmed with the tsar's spies.

It was particularly hard on the officers. They were all aristocrats, princes, counts, barons, or the darling sons of merchant families, great millionaires—a sleek, preened, fair-skinned, well-fed breed of people. And when they walked past soldiers standing to attention, they would carelessly wave a white glove, without bothering to look.

Which isn't to say that they were beastly to the soldiers—rather they would just walk past them, as though they were walking past a Morris column, past a tree or a stone. But for the slightest misdemeanour they would punish them mercilessly.

Meanwhile, the soldiers pined away; they pined for their families, for their homes, for work. "Ah, what I'd give to be working in the field right now!" the soldiers would think.

Ivan Naumenko was one such man.

You would never know to look at a man that, day and night, something was gnawing away at his heart. As always, soldiers fool around: they play leapfrog, piggyback each other, roar with laughter and play three-card Monte. While the rest of the time, in spite of the deadly heat, they stand guard in full attire.

But Naumenko himself never spared a thought for his pining; he was always good-humoured, talkative, diligent and able in his duties—he was well liked by his comrades. Even the officers singled him out, but they singled him out as they would a well-fitted saddle from one that was not.

Naumenko spared no though for his pining, but rather thought that he was onto a good thing, that he was well off here.

Only it happened that when he would stand on guard or at the listening post, and the stars would come out—oh, such big stars, the likes of which he had never seen at home in Voronezh Province—he would feel a pang in his heart.

Inland there were mountains—casting an enormous black shadow. Beyond the gardens, by the shore, the night-time sea emerged slowly and gravely, and from the gardens wafted the scent of exotic flowers. And Naumenko thought: "My Motrya must've tidied up by now, milked the cows. Everyone's gone to sleep... Ahh!"

His little lady had an upturned nose, a round face and dark brows—a sweet girl, and what a worker! They have a little girl who's just turned three. She was born just as he received his posting.

So now he lies there with a loaded rifle, keeping watch like some wild animal: mightn't someone be clambering over the wire into the imperial residence? And if he does spot someone clambering over—be it one of his own boys or an intruder—he has orders to shoot without challenge.

One day, when he had a quiet moment, Naumenko sat down on the grass under a tree and lay out some presents he had been saving up for his family: three silk kerchiefs, a coral necklace and a doll. One kerchief for old mama, one for wifey and one for his darling girl. And the necklace for his darling girl, and the doll for his darling girl too. And if you pressed the doll to your chest, it would say, "Ppa-ppa!" And its eyes would roll back. Naumenko looked at the doll and chuckled:

"A live soul! Would ya look at that..."

He had four months left, and then homeward.

Naumenko hadn't noticed the officer walking past behind him.

The officer stopped:

"Hey, you!"

Naumenko jumped to his feet, still holding the doll in his hands. The officer glowered:

"Are you blind?"

Naumenko just stood there bewildered, forgetting to throw the doll away.

The officer marched up to him and fixed his grey eyes on him, full of inexplicable hatred. Then he landed a skilful and powerful blow to Naumenko's chin, causing his head to lurch back. The diamond signet ring on the officer's finger hit Naumenko's jaw, and the salty taste of blood appeared in his mouth.

This was not a first: they would beat officers and NCOs, they would beat him and his comrades, and the soldiers would obediently keep quiet about all this; only in the barracks, when they were left alone, did they air their thoughts.

But here Naumenko himself didn't know what happened: he drew back his arm and punched the officer square in the face.

The officer turned as white as a sheet, reeling, thrust his hand in his pocket, but found his revolver missing.

He about-faced and began to skulk off, straining over his shoulder, through his teeth:

"Go and tell them you're under arrest."

Naumenko went and turned himself in.

From that point on, everything happened in accordance with the iron rule of law: interrogations, handcuffs, a trial and… a post, and nearby a freshly dug pit.

The platoon approached. Naumenko was blindfolded and placed up against the post beside the pit.

The platoon's commanding officer raised his sabre. The soldiers took aim at Naumenko's chest.

Suddenly there came a breathless cry:

"Stop!... Sto-o-op!..."

A soldier came running and shouting along the path below, waving his arms incessantly.

"Stop!... Stop!..."

Directly the mist cleared up, and everyone saw what until then had been hidden from view: a vast calm sea, a lone white sail amid its deep blue, the azure of the sky, the mountains shimmering from the heat; they heard the chirping and twittering of birds flitting about in a nearby thicket.

Naumenko stood there like a blind man, his eyes covered, yet he too did see—he saw his far-distant Voronezh Province, a white hut, Motrya and... and his darling girl with a necklace, with her coral necklace around her neck.

Somewhere in his ear, or perhaps not in his ear, but behind the ear, in his eye, or perhaps not in his eye, but... in his heart, in his heart that, so as not to give fright, was beating very softly—somewhere in his heart he began to sense "pardon... pardon".

The soldier who had come running stood to attention and, gasping for breath, gave a salute:

"Permission to report, sir!"

"What's the meaning of this?"

"It's just the quartermaster's asking that the things he's got on him need to be handed over, given there's a shortage in the storehouse—to put it plain, some have gone missing, so the quartermaster's ans—"

"What things? What on earth are you on about? I can't make out a word you're saying..."

"Permission to report, sir, that since he"—he nodded towards Naumenko—"doesn't need his clothes no more, it's all the same if he loses them, but seeing as there's a shortage in the storehouse, the quartermaster would be mighty grateful..."

"Very well," said the officer and angrily turned his back. The soldier went up to Naumenko.

"Well, brother, off with them... It's all the same now..."

Naumenko, unable to see and clumsily poking his arms about, began removing his tunic, then, fiddling about with his belt, his trousers, then one boot, then the other, and everyone watched as the clay scattered from under his foot into the pit.

The soldier took his clothing and boots and, turning to the officer with them under his arm, said:

"Sir, permission to take the underwear, too. The quartermaster gave orders..."

"Very well, just be quick about it."

"Looks like you'll have to take them off, Ivan..."

Clumsily and blindly, Naumenko began removing his shirt, then his underwear, and stood there without shame, with his arms lowered and his sallow emaciated body before everyone's eyes—with only his face hidden. The heat was shimmering, but his body was covered in goose flesh. And when the soldier saw this helpless naked body, his jaw quivered. He began rolling up the clothes, the underwear, the boots, but everything went tumbling from his hands. At last he gathered it all up under his arm and hurriedly set about slipping back down. He hadn't made it to the bend in the road when he heard the crack of a volley resounding in the mountains.

He looked round. They were hurriedly burying the pit. And so he ran down, wiping the tears from his face.

DECEMBER 1917

(Translated by Bryan Karetnyk)

DOVID BERGELSON (1884–1952)

Scenes from the Revolution

I. THE RED TRAIN

A commotion reaches us from the train car's long corridor, a clamour with the sound of running. Someone shoves open the door of our compartment while racing past and shouts:

"*Gospoda!* Gentlemen! The train is moving from the front—with a big red flag... a big red flag!"

He shouts and disappears.

We wrench ourselves from sleep—I and the passengers who had spent all night playing cards. It takes some time for us to sit back down on the bunk.

"A big red flag?..."

Astonished, as after a long daze, we look into each other's faces and see that they're crazed: there's "nothing" in our eyes—eyes full of "nothing". For the first time in our lives we have awoken to see ourselves—aged and astonished, with "nothing" in our eyes:

"A big red flag from the front?"

We have no words left for each other. We look at one another mutely, as if learning to speak. Then suddenly we all look at the tall, young blond passenger who always stammers while he speaks, and therefore always invites pity.

"*Eto nie d-d-durno!* Not b-b-bad, eh?" he blurts out happily all of a sudden.

And this too is crazy—for the first time in our lives we see that a person can match what he stammers.

We continue to sit, in our own corners, carrying within ourselves our troubled hearts. And the train—it carries on; it runs over endless snowy fields.

The train, with the big red flag from the front…

2. THE BELLYBUTTON

A short, blubbery little figure—red and sweaty. With its small, stubby feet, it bums around the festive street. It smiles with a gaping animal snout, with a torn flesh-wound circle of a mouth—its muzzle, with a hole in the middle of its disarrayed, moving teeth.

It dances luxuriously, tosses its cap to the side and stretches both its hands towards me for an embrace.

"Who are you?" I ask it.

"The Bellybutton," it answers.

"And what do you want?"

"A kiss."

"And what's the commotion?"

"Revolution!"

"And what did you do before?"

"…"

The great day has come, the day of the great holiday of freed will. Many suns light up, and among them—there it is, the eminent and eternal. The street teems with people. Celebratory faces beam. Heads crowned with flowers and banners on walls. New shouts of happiness, of a life reborn, newly dreamt up. Children dance in the streets. In fresh, white clothes, with flowers in flowing blond hair, they dance in a circle, holding one another fast. But a short, blubbery little man, red and sweaty, slips into the middle of the circle. It dances on small, stubby feet in the middle—the Bellybutton—it smiles with its gaping animal snout, with the little torn flesh-wound circle of its muzzle and stretches out its hands to hug and kiss.

In white clothes, with flowers on their heads, with their hair down, children dance in a circle.

Perhaps the children don't know that the Bellybutton dances in the middle…

APRIL–MAY 1917

(Translated by Michael Casper)

THE GUILLOTINE

The publication of *Subtly Worded*, a collection of stories and sketches by Nadezhda Teffi, finally introduced English readers to one of Russia's most important authors in translations worthy of her canny and cutting prose. As Anna Marie Jackson writes in her introduction to the volume, "Although she is still often seen primarily as a humorist, the scope of her work was, almost from the beginning, broader and deeper. As often as not, her stories are small tragedies." Indeed, Teffi's work—like that of all great tragic humorists—carries unusual weight with a spring in its step. It weds a bracing clarity of vision with a maximal subtlety of diction. Like Mark Twain, Teffi knew that "the difference between the almost right word and the right word is really a large matter—'tis the difference between the lightning-bug and the lightning." Teffi's words are always thrillingly illuminating, and often cathartic.

Born into a noble family in St Petersburg in 1872, Nadezhda Lokhvitskaya married in 1890 and moved to the country—but family life didn't suit her. She left her husband and three children and moved back to the capital in 1900, to begin a career as an author. Choosing an androgynous pseudonym, "Teffi", she soon became a popular contributor to the journals, a true literary celebrity. Famously, her admirers included both Tsar Nicholas II and Lenin. She, for her part, cast a cold eye on both the imperial social order and its sworn enemies. Teffi left Petersburg in 1919, at the height of the Civil War, travelled through present-day Ukraine, made her way to Constantinople and eventually settled in Paris in 1920, where she lived and worked until her death in 1952. She was as fine an observer of the humour and tragedy of émigré existence as she had been of life in her homeland; she remains one of the great, and most accessible, chroniclers of the tumultuous twentieth century.

The first sketch below was published in the summer of 1917, months before the Bolshevik coup. Her 'Few Words about Lenin' cut through the hypocritical bluster of a party in the minority that called itself "the majority" (the sense behind the Russian word *bolsheviki*): "if Lenin were to talk about a meeting at which he, Zinoviev, Kamenev and five horses were present, he would say: 'There were eight of us.'" It is a desperate, unusually direct plea for people to wake up, take notice of an impending threat. Her hopeful prediction that Lenin might run was, of course, wrong; the Bolsheviks did come to power, and found a different way to deal with disappointment and dissent in their ranks. 'The Guillotine', written in 1918, presents Teffi at her bleakest and most acerbic. The story is a pre-emptive "memoir" from the near future. Clearly shocked by the ease with which the Bolsheviks had managed to seize power, Teffi presents the Russian bourgeoisie as fools complicit in their own destruction. She derides their general pettiness, which manifests itself in pointless rivalry, greed and knee-jerk anti-Semitism. Not surprisingly, 'The Guillotine' didn't find a publisher in 1918—even in White-controlled Southern Russia.

TEFFI (1872–1952)

A Few Words about Lenin

The Bolsheviks are confused.

They had no idea this was going to happen. They had no idea there would be a new offensive.

But this is not a problem, really, and they shouldn't despair. After all, this is all quite in keeping with Bolshevik psychology. The Bolsheviks have always failed to sense or to predict pivotal moments in history. They have always shown a rare and quite remarkable lack of political intuition.

They have never once anticipated any important workers' movement. The best they have ever been able to do is to jump on the bandwagon after the event, a mode of operation which they themselves described ingeniously in 1905 with the term "tail-endism".

They were annoyed and ashamed to have been caught napping by Gapon's movement. But at the time, all their political energy was absorbed by the struggle with the Mensheviks, and they greeted the demise and arrest of the Menshevik organizers with pure and heartfelt joy.

"That's just fine. Let them cool their heels in prison. They can read a few books, study a little."

They only found out about Gapon on 9 January, when workers were shot outside the Winter Palace.

"Gapon? Who's Gapon? Why were the workers following him? According to Engels, armed struggle on the streets of a modern city is an impossibility."

Nevertheless, they decided to send some agitators along.

"Tail-endism!"

They sent two boys along. Then they themselves got down to the important business: lambasting the Mensheviks.

Then the red days of the first Russian Revolution dawned. Crimson flames spread over the towns and villages, alarm bells sounded, gunfire roared.

And the principles of "tail-endism" demanded that Lenin be unleashed.

The young people were excited. They awaited his arrival anxiously.

"Lenin himself! Lenin is coming! Oh, if only we live to see the day, to catch just a glimpse of him…"

"Lenin is here."

Lenin turned up his collar, hid his nose, and off he went to a meeting…

So this was Lenin!

Medium height, greyish and absolutely ordinary. Something not quite right about his forehead, though. A very protuberant, stubborn and heavy forehead. Not an inspirational forehead, not a truth-seeking forehead or a creative forehead. A forehead that looked stuffed full.

People waited to see what he would say.

And then he said it.

He said: "According to Engels, armed struggle on the streets of a modern city is an impossibility."

He said this. He said this at a time when the blazing whirlwind of the revolution was raging over the whole of Russia.

He sensed nothing, predicted nothing. He knew nothing but what he'd been stuffed with: the history of socialism.

That's how it started.

Here we have him, the true and honest prophet of the great religion of socialism. But, unfortunately, a tongue of fire from the

Holy Spirit has never come to rest on this apostle. He has never had any inspiration, flight or fire.

Every bit of him is tightly stuffed, like a leather football, squeaking and cracking at the seams, but unable to fly into the air unless it is kicked.

This lack of sensitivity could explain why *agents provocateurs* have easily found a place side by side with the most honest Bolsheviks.

This could also explain the utter tactlessness of the "sealed carriage".

Engels couldn't have foreseen that sealed carriage, and wasn't able to give instructions.

As for *agents provocateurs*, it isn't enough simply to hear what they say: their words and deeds will always be in line with, or even go beyond, the most striking slogans of the party they are engaged in manipulating; what is important is to *feel* what they are saying and doing. People who do not have this sensitivity will always be surprised by events that they have completely failed to predict.

Isn't the word "Bolshevik" now completely, irrevocably discredited?

Every pickpocket who takes a wallet from some heedless passer-by can now say that he's a follower of Lenin.

"Why not? Lenin takes somebody else's house, a pickpocket takes somebody else's wallet. The only difference is one of scale. After all, great ships need deep waters."

Leninists, Bolsheviks, anarcho-communists, heavies, convicted housebreakers. What a mess! What a witch's brew!

What a huge task—to raise up, to clean the great idea of socialism of all this rubbish!

The Bolsheviks want to take stock of their supporters right across the board. To gladden their hearts.

I had often heard Leninists speak at minor street demonstrations. And I have always been struck by what an impressively fine lot their supporters are.

Once, on the memorable night after the Milyukov note, some Bolshevik was standing on the corner of Sadovaya Street, calling for an end to annexations and war indemnity. A young soldier standing beside me was displaying fervent support for the speaker, roaring, shaking his fist and rolling his eyes.

So I listened, trying to make out what the soldier was shouting:

"We don't need Anne Exations! To hell with her! They're not going to bring in that woman again. Down with Anne Exations, to hell with her!"

They're not going to bring in that woman again.

The soldier honestly thought that Anne Exations was some woman who was going to be brought in. What's more, this was about to happen again. Apparently, Anne Exations had been brought in before.

A tall Ukrainian soldier was standing at the centre of another knot of people assuring them that all government ministers had to be driven out, or the "reactionary hydra would again raise its head".

And next to them stood an old woman, wiping her tears and repeating over and over in a beseeching voice:

"Poor dear, God grant her peace, the Lord help her, oh, the suffering she's seen…"

It all sounds like a comic sketch made up for the papers, but, I swear, it was stupider than anything anyone could have thought up.

Here it was, a public declaration by one part of Lenin's great army—a declaration of its ideology.

But, actually, Lenin is happy with his army. Happy with the old woman praying for the hydra of reactionism. Happy with the soldier who didn't want "that woman brought in again". He is even content with Malinovsky. And with the few dozen convicted housebreakers he has on his side—his "specialists". He does not disavow them.

A great, triumphal procession of illiterate fools and wilful criminals.

Anybody who wants to work less and eat more can call himself a Leninist with confidence.

We demand clear and equal grub for all!

Any horse would subscribe to that slogan and would follow after any owner who proclaimed it.

And, actually, if Lenin were to talk about a meeting at which he, Zinoviev, Kamenev and five horses were present, he would say: "There were eight of us."

So how are the Bolsheviks going to get out of this?

Will Lenin, perhaps, turn his collar up again, hide his nose and go back to Switzerland?

Because they'll have to get out of it somehow. Those committed workers who have been on their side up until now will not want to stay when they see themselves in the company of horses.

For centuries now, people have laughed at the prank played by the emperor Caligula, who brought a horse into the Senate.

But, after all, a single horse, and in the Senate at that, is far less of a discredit to a cause than a whole herd, propping up the great cause of socialism.

JUNE 1917

(Translated by Rose France)

The Guillotine

I dedicate these memoirs to Trotsky, with heartfelt gratitude.

As I would not be able to write these memoirs after being guillotined, I am forced to write them now.

Still, it really doesn't matter: I noticed some time ago that my actual future usually turns out to be almost identical to my dreams of the future. So I write these memoirs of the future safe in the knowledge that this is just how it will be.

* * *

In the evening, just as we were about to have supper, Vera Valeryanovna called in.

"I can only stay a minute," she said. "I'm in a dreadful hurry."

"What's the rush?" we said. "Stay awhile!"

"No, I can't. I'm in a hurry. I only popped in to say goodbye. I'm due to be guillotined tomorrow."

"But Vera, darling!" we exclaimed. "What a wonderful coincidence! We're all scheduled for tomorrow!"

"Spend the night at my place," I said. "We can all go together. You don't want to go all the way from Galernaya Street to Palace Square. It's a lot closer from here. And tonight we can eat the last of the strawberry jam."

She wasn't to be persuaded easily.

"You know how it is; there's always so much to do at the last minute…"

But I was delighted. We'd have a grand time together. After all, it's not much fun waiting for three hours for your turn to come round.

The day before, apparently, the chopping personnel had gone on strike for better wages and left people standing about in the freezing cold until five o'clock.

A delegation from the choppers had appealed to the condemned for support. Naturally, the condemned were sympathetic: they promised that, if worst came to worst, they too would go on strike, refusing to be executed until the government had conceded to the choppers' demands. And by five o'clock the whole incident had been dealt with decisively.

But these queues are really quite outrageous! You have a line on one side stretching almost as far as Nevsky Prospect, a line on the other up to Palace Bridge, and a third winding right round the back of the Hermitage. Despite the latest technology and the electric motor, the guillotine works slowly. What's the point of being able to lop off five hundred heads at once if you still have to lay all those five hundred people into position first? People pushing and shoving—utter chaos! The wait is never less than two hours, and in the freezing cold. The crowd starts complaining, muttering.

"They squeeze us for taxes, but they can't organize anything properly. So much for all this talk of strong government. Put a fool in charge and you'll be the first to suffer."

They do have a point. Would it really be so difficult to issue people with cards? Or to put up district guillotines?

We sat around talking till midnight, swapping all sorts of funny stories. Apparently, certain fashionable Russian ladies have devised a special wig "à la Marie Antoinette" for the guillotine. The wigs cost a fortune. But is it really worth it? The wigs lose their curl in the damp air, and, in any case, the whole thing just looks daft—imagine, some Marie Antoinette standing in a queue.

It was different during the French Revolution. Back then, a woman went up on the scaffold as if it were a stage. The crowd would be watching—she would be seen by everyone.

In those days, ordinary people were fascinated by the guillotine: it frightened and attracted them. The man who invented it seemed to them a mysterious and marvellous creature.

Boys on the street would sing songs about him:

> *Guillotin,*
> *Médecin,*
> *Politique...*

The executioner was also a notable person, an object of universal interest.

"Monsieur de Paris."

But things are different now. The guillotine is set up like a factory machine, operated by workers. It's all so clear and simple.

And all these bourgeois pretensions, seeking to lend the affair an air of beauty and solemnity, are just plain silly. When, oh, when will we finally grow up and adopt the correct attitude towards the everyday details of modern life?

The Russian people got used to the guillotine so quickly, feel so much at ease with it, that it's hard to believe there was ever a time when we didn't have it.

They treat the guillotine with that affectionate warmth so unique to the Russian people, calling it "Gallotina Ivanovna".

Now you can hear a new verse in the popular street songs, the *chastushki*:

> If you don't get up this morning
> Bake me up a birthday pie
> Off I go to Gallotina
> You can wave my head goodbye!

We got up early the next morning.

Vera Valeryanovna was right. There is always a great deal to do at the last minute.

At nine o'clock, Michel, a family friend, knocked on the door. He had managed to swap places with a colleague—now he could be guillotined with us.

By the time we had had a cup of tea and something to eat, the clock had struck ten and it was time to get ready.

Michel is an absolute treasure: he had made sandwiches for the journey.

"We may have to wait three hours in the queue," he said. "We'll get hungry."

Off we went. Not a cab to be found, of course. And all the trams were full to bursting. So we set off on foot along Sadovaya Street.

"Awful!" grumbled Vera Valeryanovna. "Bad luck at the start. That doesn't bode well."

She's rather superstitious, you see.

At last, near Sennaya Square, we came across a cab driver.

"How much?" we asked.

"Thirty roubles."

"Are you mad?" we protested. "We're not off on some jaunt, you know. We're going on important business. To be guillotined."

"It's all the same to me," whined a beard from under a hat. "It's all one to me, wherever I take yous. Some might look on it different, and pay extra, seeing as it's the last time they take a cab."

"And just why should we pay you extra?"

"It's all right for some," muttered the beard. "Yous are all getting your heads chopped off and that's the end of it. Some of us have to work. Some of us have horses to feed. Oats don't come cheap these days, you know…"

"Take twenty roubles," Michel tried to beat him down. "And if you drive well, you'll get something extra."

"I know your sort," said the cab driver, now in a nasty mood. "I'm the one who loses out, giving rides to yous condemned. Had one in my cab the other day. Kept talking about the nice tip he'd give me. So I took him to the guillotine, and he goes, 'Wait here, I have to get some change. All I have is a million-rouble note,' and then he dives into the crowd. So I wait and I wait till I get sick of waiting, and I get down and go off to look for him. I'm asking around, 'Hey, citizens, anyone seen a dark fellow in a brown cap?' And everyone starts laughing. 'It's not him, by any chance, is it?' I look and there he is—already got himself executed, his head lying there in the snow!"

The cab driver's funny story put us in a happier mood. The next minute another cab turned up, and we set off.

There were masses of people on Palace Square. Carriages, motor cars, pedestrians. But there wasn't much in the way of pushing and shoving. This was probably thanks to Trotsky's proclamations, plastered all over the walls, stating that those to be guillotined were themselves responsible for maintaining order.

We paid the cab driver and gave him a tip. He told us to "break a leg".

There were so many people we knew! In one queue we saw Olga Nikolaevna and Natalia Mikhailovna, both in wigs "à la Marie Antoinette", though for some reason the wigs weren't powdered, but ginger. Their faces were blue with cold, and it's fair to say that the overall effect was not a pretty sight.

A clean-shaven man was putting on quite a show for the crowd. People said he was a compère from some minor theatre.

Newspaper boys were nipping about among the queues, together with vendors of *sbiten* and fried pies. Michel wanted to try one, but I talked him out of it—such filthy things, smelling of tallow candles.

There was a bit of a scene in one of the queues. A nimble young man with dark hair had managed to jump the queue and get himself executed before those around him even knew what was happening.

There was no end of fuss! People were shouting that bribes had changed hands, and wasn't that just typical of the Jews, always sneaking to the front of the queue?

It was getting cold. We were bored.

Michel asked us to save his place in the queue and went up to have a closer look at the guillotine. He was concerned that the opening for the heads wasn't big enough.

"I've got a big head. All in all, I'm a big chap!" he said. "I'm afraid I'll scrape my ears."

Nearby, two ladies were having a tiff.

"How can you douse yourself in perfume like that before the guillotine? It's absolutely not on, I tell you! Now I have a migraine coming on."

"Well, well, aren't we sensitive?" snorted the other. "Don't worry, my dear, your migraine won't have a chance to come on."

She was right.

The doors of the enclosure around the guillotine were thrown open and our queue began to stream forward.

"Now, now—no pushing!"

"Show a bit of manners!"

"Honestly, this crowd."

"Such inconsiderate types. We condemned ought to take things into our own hands. We should form a union. Why should it only be other people who enjoy the perks of being guillotine operators?"

"It's too late now."

"What were we thinking of earlier?"

"Keep moving, now, keep moving. Don't hold everybody up."

"We're coming. We're coming."

1918

(Translated by Rose France)

APOCALYPSE

Vasily Rozanov (1856–1919), a religious philosopher who advocated sexual liberation, published wildly contradictory pronouncements in conservative and liberal periodicals (the latter under a pseudonym) and was so enamoured of Dostoyevsky that he styled himself "the Underground Man" and married the older writer's troubled mistress, Polina Suslova (1839–1918), was perhaps the most eccentric Russian thinker of his era—an era rich in eccentrics. Rozanov's parents died when he was still a boy, and he was raised by his older brother, a schoolteacher, whose job required the siblings to move from their native Betluga to Simbirsk, and later to Nizhny Novgorod. In 1882 Rozanov graduated from Moscow University and became a teacher himself, taking up posts at *gymnasia* in Simbirsk and other provincial towns.

In the 1890s his writings on Dostoyevsky, Orthodoxy and politics began to spark the interest of leading intellectuals. After the appearance of his article denouncing the Russian educational system in 1893, he was forced to leave his job, but, with the help of his publishers, was able to find a governmental post in St Petersburg. There he co-founded the Religious-Philosophical Society, attended not only by religious philosophers like Nikolay Berdyaev (1874–1948), but by future politicos like Kerensky, and by Symbolist poets like Zinaida Gippius and Alexander Blok (see pp. 18, 46–48). Rozanov's work was programmatically irrational, mercurial, fragmentary; he was, by turns, reactionary and progressive, pious and blasphemous, philo- and anti-Semitic. What he claimed to value most was vitality, be it in the realms of social and sexual relations, religious experience or the written word. He is best known for his collections *Solitaria* (1912) and *Fallen Leaves* (2 vols., 1913, 1915), which capture the living movement of his thought in provocative, kaleidoscopic collages. In the summer of 1917, Rozanov, his second (common-law) wife and their children fled the chaos of revolutionary Petrograd and moved into the house of a seminary teacher in the town of Sergiyev Posad, some forty miles to the north of Moscow. The ageing firebrand regarded the February and October Revolutions not simply as disasters, but as the end of the old world and everything associated with it. Ailing and starving, he spent the last year of his life composing *The Apocalypse of Our Time*, which appeared in ten pamphlets between November 1917 and October 1918.

Alexey Remizov (1877–1957), among the greatest experimental prose stylists of the twentieth century, rivalled his older colleague in eccentricity. He was instantly drawn to Rozanov upon first meeting him in St Petersburg in 1905. He had just moved there after eight years of internal exile. Remizov was born into a Moscow merchant-class family, received a technical education, and enrolled at Moscow University's Faculty of Physics and Mathematics in 1895. The following year he was arrested, apparently mistakenly, for confronting police during a demonstration, and exiled to Penza, where he was rearrested two years later and sentenced to another term in Vologda. Remizov had begun writing in the provinces, but it was only after his move to the capital that he devoted himself to literature, developing an idiosyncratic prose technique that blended archaic and highly colloquial syntax and diction, often relying on folkloric and religious models and modes of narration. His work is linguistically vibrant, mercurial, fragmentary; in short, it bears more than a passing resemblance to that of Rozanov. The younger eccentric was extremely fond of his path-breaking predecessor and even inducted him into the exclusive "Great and Free Order of the Apes" (*Obezvolpal*), which he founded in 1907. In 1919 Remizov published a brief, poignant obituary of Rozanov, in which he called him "the most vital of our older contemporaries, all-embracing, one of a kind in Russian literature, and alone in our wandering life". Later, in 1923, two years after leaving Russia, he published a memoir of their friendship, imitating Rozanov's own cantankerous, erratic prose style.

Like Rozanov, Remizov perceived the events of 1917 through an apocalyptic lens. His 'Lay of the Ruin of Rus', which was likely written in the weeks before the October Revolution, is modelled on an eponymous thirteenth-century text lamenting a crushing military defeat at the hands of Batu Khan, which marked the beginning of 240 years of Mongol rule. Rozanov's *Apocalypse* and Remizov's 'Lay' differ in vision: for Rozanov, the current catastrophe speaks to the failure of Christianity as such, whereas for Remizov it is the Russians who are to blame for abandoning their faith. Both these works fed into Blok's epic poem *The Twelve* (see pp. 50–63), in which the poet comes to a different conclusion.

After settling in France in 1923, Remizov continued to ruminate on Russia's past and on its literary tradition, but his work—immensely influential before the revolution—attracted less and less attention.

Near the end of his life in Paris he felt so isolated that he applied for and received Soviet citizenship, though he never did return to Russia; this desperate act only served to anger and alienate his fellow émigrés all the more. He died lonely and blind, an exile among exiles.

VASILY ROZANOV (1856–1919)

from The Apocalypse of Our Time

TO THE READER

S tarting on 15 November [1917], I shall publish every two weeks or every month pieces under the general title "Apocalypse of Our Time". In view of current events, whose apocalyptic character is not just apparent but real, the title needs no explanation. There is no doubt that the profound cause of all that is happening now lies in the fact that in European (and not just Russian) society great voids have appeared where Christianity once was, and everything is falling into these voids: thrones, classes, ranks, labour, wealth. Everything has been undermined, everyone has been undermined. Everyone is perishing, everything is perishing. But all of this falls into the void of a soul that has lost its ancient substance.

HOW ARE WE DYING?

What then? Death has come, and therefore the time for death has come.

Death, the grave of one-sixth of the earth's surface. "The simple ethnographic existence of the former Russian Tsardom and Empire", about which people are already talking and giving lectures, about which one can think, with which indeed people are reconciling themselves. The *former* Rus is being transformed into something like the "Polabian Slavs".

"Former Rus"—how can one say this? But it is already being said.

It is not death that is sad. "A man dies not when he has reached ripeness, but when his time has come"—that is, when his vital fluids have reached the point where death becomes necessary and inevitable.

If every man's death is "willed by God", how could we accept or believe that the death of a nation or a kingdom is not "willed by God"? That is the real question. It means that God did not wish there to be a Rus any more. He drives it out of the sunlight. "Depart, you unnecessary people."

Why are we "unnecessary"?

For a long time we have been writing in our "golden literature" of the "Diary of a Superfluous Man", "Notes of an Unnecessary Man"—or "of an Idle Man". We have invented all kinds of "undergrounds"... We have hidden ourselves somehow from the light of the sun, as if we were ashamed of ourselves.

If a man is ashamed of himself—won't the sun be ashamed of him too? Man and the sun are bound together.

So we are "unnecessary" under the sun, and we go off into a kind of night. Night. Non-being. The grave.

We die like braggarts, like actors. "No cross, no prayers." If there is someone at whose death there is no cross or prayers, it is the Russians. How strange! All our lives we crossed ourselves, muttered prayers, then suddenly death comes and we throw away the cross. "It's simply that the Russians never lived like Orthodox believers." The move to socialism, and so to atheism, took place as easily among the peasants and soldiers as "going to the bath-house and splashing fresh water on themselves". That's exactly how it was, that's reality, not some crazy nightmare.

So what in fact are we dying of? No, really, how can it be explained in one word, condensed into a single point? We are dying from just one fundamental cause: *lack of self-respect*. In fact we are killing ourselves. It is not so much that the sun is driving us away. We are driving ourselves away. "Get lost, you devil!"

Nihilism… That's what it is, nihilism—a name that Russians have long been using to baptize themselves or, rather, to debaptize themselves.

—Who are you? You, wandering about in the sun?

—I am a nihilist.

—I only *pretended* to be praying.

—I only pretended to be *living in the kingdom*.

—In reality I'm my own man.

—I work in a pipe factory, I don't care about the rest.

—I want to work as little as possible.

—I want to have as much fun as possible.

—And I don't want to go to war.

And the soldier throws away his rifle. The worker leaves his bench.

—Let the land bring forth food on its own.

And he leaves the land.

—We all know the land is God's. It belongs to everyone equally.

Yes, but you're not a man of God. And the land in which you put your trust won't give you anything. And because it won't give you anything, you'll paint it red with blood.

There is Cain's land, and there is Abel's land. And your land, Russians, is Cain's. You have cursed your land, and your land has cursed you. That's nihilism and its workings.

And the sun doesn't shine on the man of darkness. It doesn't need the man of darkness.

It's remarkable, how we go to the grave in a state of intoxication. We began the war self-intoxicated: do you remember that month of August, the meeting of the tsar with his people, where everything was false to the core? And the victories—the most memorable being the victory of the Cossack Kryuchkov, who, as usual, chopped off seven German heads. And that brave Menshevik slogan—"We must win".

And Dolina, with her victory concerts, first at the Ciniselli Circus, then at Tsarskoe Selo. But why this "we must win"? Victory is not created in wartime, but in peacetime. And in peacetime we did nothing, and if there was one thing we knew full well, it was that we weren't doing anything. But then—things got even better. If there was something we got carried away by, it was revolution. "The complete satisfaction of our desires." No, really, what else could we want? "When the thirsty man has drunk his fill and the hungry man eaten his fill, then we'll have revolution." And now, before the revolutionary has worn out his first pair of boots, he collapses into the grave. Isn't he just an actor, a show-off? And where are our prayers? Where are our crosses? "There isn't a priest who'd give a burial to a corpse like that."

He's a witch, a werewolf, not a living being. There's no living soul in him and never has been.

—A nihilist.

They don't give nihilists a Christian burial. They steer clear: "Devil take him!"

His life was accursed; so is his death.

One-sixth of the dry land. An intoxicated revolution, as the war was an intoxicated war. "We shall conquer." You bet! So isn't it a strange fact, that one-sixth of the earth's surface produced just thistles and thorns up to the day when the sun said, "I don't need you," "I'm fed up with shining on an empty land"?

Nihilism—"What grows out of you?"

—Nothing.

There's no point in talking about "nothing".

—We did not respect ourselves. The essence of Russia is lack of self-respect.

It's obvious. You can respect labour and sweat, but we neither laboured nor sweated. And because we neither laboured nor sweated, the earth threw us off, the planet threw us off.

Did we deserve it?

And how!

To exist for a thousand years, to live through princedoms and kingdoms and empires, to have dealings with everyone, to wear plumage and hats, to put on a God-fearing appearance: while in reality, to curse, to curse ourselves as "nihilists" (because in normal language that is a curse), and to die.

Russia is like a fake general for whom a fake priest sings a requiem. "Really, this was an actor who'd run away from a provincial theatre."

★ ★ ★

The most astonishing thing, which reveals the essence of the whole business, is the fact that "in reality, nothing has happened". "But—everything has collapsed." What happened to bring down the kingdom? It just fell one day. Just an ordinary weekday, like any other day: not a Sunday, or a Saturday, or even a Muslim Friday. God just spat and blew out the candle. There was no food, and queues formed outside the shops. Yes, there was an opposition. Yes, the tsar threw a fit. But when in Rus was there enough of anything if it hadn't been for the work of Jews and Germans? When did we not have an opposition? When did the tsar not throw fits? O melancholy Friday, or Monday, or Tuesday...

How can you die in such a sad, sordid, stinking way?—"An actor would at least have made a scene. After all, you were always ready to play Hamlet." "Do you remember your lines? And even Leonid Andreyev had nothing to spit out. Prose, nothing but prose."

Yes, if there was ever a "tedious affair", it is "the fall of Rus".

The candle was blown out. And it wasn't even God, but... some drunken woman who tripped up and fell flat. Stupid. Foul. "Don't give us a tragedy, give us a vaudeville."

★ ★ ★

A PASSAGE FOR *APOCALYPSE* THAT REMAINED IN MANUSCRIPT:

THE CANDLE

Russia is a changeling.

She was changed for a candle that burned differently, with a different flame, a non-Russian light that won't warm a Russian hut.

Who brought it, and was it long ago? The Decembrists maybe, or Herzen, or Belinsky? Or maybe Peter? But from the 1860s it was clear that Russia's light had gone. Now there is only hot wax on the candlestick, running down, unsightly...

But when the alien candle burns down (and it too will burn down in accordance with the laws of history), we shall gather up from the candlestick the remains of the old Russian wax. And we'll make a new thin candle, a two-copeck affair. But we'll hold it in our hands, even if it's old and decrepit. And let this be the dying candle that the sick man holds in his hands. And we shall hold it and we shall die.

1917–18

(Translated by Peter France)

ALEXEY REMIZOV (1877–1957)

The Lay of the Ruin of Rus

I

B road Rus of the open fields, motherland of mine, you who have suffered much hardship, much passion, I see you abandoning the light of life, cast down in the fire.

There were work days, days of toil and of harvest, and there were feast days with long all-night services, the saying of mass, then the loud choral dance, its noise and its swinging.

There was hunger, there was also abundance.

There was punishment, there was also pardon.

There was torture, there were also great deeds, sacrifice of the self for the good of the people.

Where are they now, our deeds and our sacrifices?

The smell of smoke and the howling of apes.

Mad horseman, you want to leap over the sea from the yellow fogs of your beloved granite city, indestructible and strong like the rock of Peter—above the Neva like a whirlwind you stand, I see you in dream and in waking.

Mad brother—alack the day!—your Russia has perished.

Like a cuckoo I cry in your deserted wood, where the fallen leaves are rotting: my Russia has perished.

There were Troubles, there were Pretenders—the ex-monk and the thief—rebellion tore the land of Rus, the land fell apart, but again rose up, and again Rus was straight as an arrow, the people of

Rus rose up for the land of Rus, they saved you, they drove out your brother and cleansed the fair-sounding Kremlin—the fraternal yoke of a foreign faith was not to be endured.

There was the faith of Rus, as it had been from the beginning.

Great is the knowledge of the Volga forests down to the Iron Gates, many burning prayers they have heard, as people burned themselves in their huts for the Russian faith.

Where are you now, native stronghold, Ultimate Rus?

I cannot hear your voice, no, the smell of burning huts does not reach me from the Volga forests.

Or have your true sons submitted to fate and gone out into mother-wilderness?

Or are the free and fearless fires of Ultimate Rus no longer to be found in Rus?

There was a Cain in Rus, a faithless man who betrayed his people, but even he in his accursed sinfulness loved his mother Rus—and made up deathless songs:

"'Twas near Moscow, 'twas near Trinity, near Sergey…"

Or another song, one to take with you to the stake:

"Do not rustle, dear mother, green oakwood…"

II

Broad Rus of open fields, I see your fair-sounding Kremlin, your gold-roofed Cathedral of the Annunciation, snowy-white like a fair maiden's breast, but no silver bell greets me, no fair-sounding peal.

Or is it drowned out by the whistle of intolerable bullets rendering pitiless the whole world's heart, the whole of the earth?

All I hear is the howling of apes.

You are burning—Rus is in flames—ash is flying.

But until now we always knew: we could be sure—you stand,

you will stand, broad Rus of open fields, unshakeable through every hardship and passion.

And even if your body is covered with scabby scales, the wild wind will blow the scabby scales from you, and once again, bright, even brighter, joyful, even more joyful, you will rise above your dense forests and above the wild grass of your steppes.

So it was, so we thought, and so our faith in you grew stronger.

Godless man-fighters who dreamt of creating an earthly paradise, men and women who were righteous in their love of humanity, leaders of people who wished them only happiness, you did your work and, little by little, uprooted the faith in doing it, not seeing that the very life of Rus was perishing with the faith.

Now Rus is rotten to the core.

Blind leaders, what have you wrought?

The blood shed on fraternal fields made the human heart pitiless, and you robbed the people of Rus of their soul.

And so I hear the howling of apes.

My Rus, you are burning!

My Rus, you have fallen and cannot be raised up, cannot raise yourself up!

My Rus, land of Rus, defenceless motherland, made pitiless by the blood of the fraternal fields, set on fire, you are burning!

III

Oh, my doomed motherland, you have stumbled, you, the unshakeable, and your imperial purple has slipped from your shoulders.

For what sin, for what mortal fault?

Is it for breaking your oath like a rotten reed and losing your ultimate faith, or is it for the blood that was shed in fraternal fields, or for untruth—the wide-open heart has more than once cried to all

Rus: "there is no truth in the lands of Rus"—or is it for your mindless, age-old silence?

Even now, humiliated, trampled underfoot, when your shrine is kicked and mocked, even now you are mute.

The mindless silence of your true sons cries out to God like a mortal sin.

Oh, my homeland, cast down, you stretch out your arms—

Or have you been visited by the wrath of God—has God raised his sword against you?

Oh, my unfortunate motherland, your calamity, your ruin, your fall are a visitation of God. Be humble to the end, accept your calamity—not calamity, but the grace of God—and your passions will cleanse you, will whiten your soul.

Let me tell you with all my pain: I do not wish you ill, but only goodness and peace—my heart is not in it—what can I say in defence of my people? And I am ashamed—I am a Russian, a son of Rus.

Oh, my miserable motherland, my humiliated mother.

I touch your wounds, your burning brow, your caked lips, your heart bursting with injury and grief, your eyes lashed with whips—

More than once I renounced you in days gone by, in the despair of my suffocating heart, I cursed you with the terrible words of Ivan the Terrible for your sedition, your falsehood.

"I am no Russian, there is no truth in the land of Rus."

But not now—I shall not desert you in your sin, in your calamity, free and captive, released and bound, holy and sinful, light and dark.

Is it for me to desert you—me, a Russian, a son of Rus, the fruit of your womb?

From my cradle I gazed at your silent stars, heard the rustle of your forests, grieved with you to the howling of your blizzards, flew with your evil spirits over your wild mountains and the boundless Gogolian steppes.

How could I abandon you?

I brought you costly adornments so that you should be still brighter, more joyful. I threaded your precious stones, the pearls of your words, on a necklace for your tender breast.

Oh, my motherland, doomed and punished, endowed with a cruel grace for the purity of your heart, you lie cast down on the greensward, I see you in the smoke of bonfires beneath bullets, and your plaits are spread out on the earth.

I shall kindle the lamp of my tireless faith, in the long hard nights I shall listen to your voice, sacred Rus of mine, to your grieving, your groans, your lamenting.

Even cast down, atoning for your sins, you will remain for ever in my heart.

As you sink to the depths you are bright.

Oh, my doomed motherland, punished by God, visited by God!

Your name will be wiped out, you will perish, and who will remember you ever existed?

I shall keep my Russian soul and my faith in your tireless truth, I shall preserve it in my heart, preserve your memory, as long as my words—your speech—survives on the suffering, cross-bearing earth, gone silent without heroism or sacrifice, bereft of song.

IV

Destitute and dumb, I stand in the wilderness where once there was Russia.

My soul is sullen.

All that I had they have stolen, they have stripped my clothes from me.

What do I need? I do not know.

I need nothing. There is nothing to live for.

Anger seethes in the soul, seethes helplessly: half my life was given to a Russia that has now become nothing, but might have been everything.

I want captivity, not liberty. I want slavery, not fraternity. I want bonds, not violence.

I am sick of man's vanity, flattery, stray, empty words.

My grief is boundless.

In Russia no faith remains, no church—can there be a church that exalts what exists in time?

And time is no more, it is gone, time is finished.

To perish is not terrible, but man cannot die in his own name alone. For there is nothing else to die for, all has perished.

And from the abyss, the angel of evil arises—a five-pointed silver star shines over his head with seven rays, and he is terrible.

"Perish in my name!"

And there is no salvation from on high.

My anger is fierce.

And the sullen blind soul reaches out with dumb arms, she reaches into infinity—

And I curse no one, for I know the hour and the date, the fulfilment of the time of fate.

Nothing will escape ruin.

Oh, if it could be avoided!

Every man alone bears the burden of his curse, the covered vessel of his soul, and he fears to spill it.

Darkness above and below.

And the heaven was rolled up like a scroll.

And there is no God.

He has hidden Himself in the scroll with the stars and the sun and the moon.

A black abyss has opened above and below.

And the devil has lost his purpose, he has hanged himself on Judas' aspen.

Yet, for some reason, all are still living.

And the louder man cries, the more terrible it is for him.

They are as children who have lost their mother.

And they do not understand the grief that is given them.

Soon the last hour will come, soon it will ring out.

A quarter to twelve.

Listen! There is nothing, no Kremlin, no Russia—just a flat empty space.

Come here and build! Let anyone who wants come and do his work—raise up a new Russia where the old one has burnt.

And forget what is old, what has been.

Try to raise up Kitezh with nets—the lake is empty, there is nothing.

A single ending without end.

V

Russian people, what have you done?

You sought happiness and you lost everything. You turned foolish, flopped like a pig into dung.

You came to believe—

Whom did you come to believe? Go on, blame yourself, pay your debts.

You forgot the land that was your cradle.

Where is your Russia?

An empty space.

Russian people, that is your unpardonable sin.

And where is your conscience, your wisdom, your cross?

I was proud to be a Russian, I guarded and cherished the name of my motherland, I prayed to holy Rus.

Now despised, with all my people, I pay the price, pitiful, poor and naked.

I dare not lift my eyes.

"Lord, what have I done!"

There is just one consolation, one hope: I shall patiently bear the burden of my days, I shall cleanse my heart and my muddied mind, and, if such is my lot, I shall rise up on the Day of Light.

Russian people, the Day of Light will come.

Can you hear the snorting of the horse?

The mad horseman who wants to leap over the sea from the yellow fogs, he crushed old Rus, he will raise up a new one, new and free, from the void.

I hear the rustle of wings above my head.

It is the new Rus, beautiful and free, my empress.

Russian people, believe, the Day of Light will come.

VI

I shall fly from the cliff like a heavy dark bird, glide motionless on my wings, gaze with eyes of glass into infinity, fly into thick darkness so as not to see a thing.

Understand me, our life drags on with great effort.

Stop, then, cleanse your hands—they are covered in blood—and your face—it is sullied by gunpowder smoke.

The earth has gone, it has shifted.

The earth is going away—

I am flying in boundless space.

The earth rested on three whales. There was chaos, but also a foundation: merchants traded, farmers ploughed, soldiers fought, workers worked.

All is topsy-turvy.

I am flying in boundless space.

To give up the life of the senses, to enter a world of air, who can do this? All that remains is to fall like a worm and to crawl.

I overtake aeroplanes.

The roar of the engines sounds in my ears.

I would crow like a cock, but I have no head; it was chopped off long ago!

Understand me, to be a stranger in one's land, not abroad, is a curse.

And that curse is my lot.

VII

All is ruined, an empty space, only a table remains—a great table at full human height.

Greedily, howling like apes and roaring with laughter, the people, grown brazen, are tearing to pieces a pie—a pie baked by Rus, now deceased—a pie of farewell, of remembrance.

They tear it, they swallow it, they choke.

And with bloodshot eyes they gnaw at the table as hungry horses gnaw at the trough. And they try to wolf it all down before the guests arrive, the future masters of the earth, who will settle on the broad Russian land.

"E-ter-nal me-mo-ry..."

1917

(Translated by Peter France)

OF DRAGONS AND MEN

Yefim Zozulya's (1891–1941) name is now all but forgotten, but he was one of the best-known satirists of the 1920s. Raised in a Jewish family in what is now Łódź, Poland, and Odessa, Ukraine, he made his debut as a journalist and humorist in 1911. He moved to Petrograd in 1914 and his first book, *The Death of the Capital*, appeared in 1918; the collection's title story is a dystopian fable in which citizens trade their freedom for peace. Although Zozulya was a leftist and became an important literary functionary in the burgeoning Soviet regime, co-founding the illustrated magazine *Ogonyok* (*Little Flame*) in 1923, his fantasies of the late 1910s and early 1920s were often censured by dogmatic Soviet critics, ostensibly for their avoidance of Soviet reality. And it is indeed difficult to read 'The Story of Ak and Humanity' (1919) as a fantasy divorced from the reality of its time, or as simply a satire on bourgeois pettiness; it is, first and foremost, a stirring protest against the arbitrariness of dictatorial rule, and one can certainly draw parallels between the directives of Ak's

Council of Public Welfare and the campaign of Red Terror initiated by the Bolsheviks against their real and perceived opponents in 1918. Zozulya continued to write and publish throughout the 1920s but was much less active in the 1930s. After the outbreak of the Second World War, he volunteered to serve, fought on the front lines before being assigned to a military newspaper, fell ill, and died in hospital on 3 November 1941.

Alexander Berkman's adaptation of Zozulya's story originally appeared in the June 1935 issue of *Esquire* magazine as 'The Dictator', by "Yefim Sosulya". His alterations (for example, swapping "billiards" for "baseball") reflect his desire to bring the story's moral closer to home for his mostly American audience; they all but declare, "It can happen here!" I have edited Berkman's adaptation only slightly, restoring a few excised passages and smoothing out a line or two. Despite—or perhaps because of—its departures, Berkman's version captures the sharp, lively tone of Zozulya's original fable. Berkman clearly felt an affinity for the tale, having witnessed the events that inspired its black humour with his own eyes.

Born in 1870 to a Jewish family in the Russian Empire, in what is now Vilnius, Lithuania, Berkman emigrated to the United States at the age of eighteen and was soon swept up in the anarchist movement, finding a political and romantic soulmate in Emma Goldman (1869–1940), another Jewish émigré from what is now Lithuania. In 1892 he was sentenced to fourteen years in prison for a failed assassination attempt on a prominent industrialist. He shaped his prison diary into an influential book, publishing it after his release, and edited two anarchist journals—*Mother Earth* and *The Blast*—before being arrested again in 1917, along with Goldman, for conspiring against the draft. During the Red Scare that followed the Bolshevik revolution, the US authorities rounded up over two hundred radical leftists, including Berkman and Goldman, and deported them to

Soviet Russia. Berkman's memoir of his Soviet sojourn, *The Bolshevik Myth* (1925), and Goldman's *My Disillusionment in Russia* (1923) and *My Further Disillusionment in Russia* (1924), chronicle just that: two radical leftists' disenchantment with the turn the revolution had taken. In his book, Berkman recalls a conversation he had with a young Chekist:

> His stories dealt mostly with the activities of the [Cheka], sudden raids, arrests and executions. He impressed me as a convinced and sincere Communist, ready to lay down his life for the Revolution. But he thought of the latter as a simple matter of extermination, with the [Cheka] as the ruthless sword. He had no conception of revolutionary ethics or spiritual values. Force and violence were to him the acme of revolutionary activity, the alpha and omega of the proletarian dictatorship. "Revolution is a prize fight," he would say, "either we win or lose. We must destroy every enemy, root every counter-revolutionist out of his lair. Sentimentalism, bosh! Every means and method is good to accomplish our purpose. What's the use of having a Revolution unless you use your best effort to make a success of it? The Revolution would be dead long ago if not for us. The [Cheka] is the very soul of the Revolution."

This is the unsentimental conviction of Ak's Council of Public Welfare. And here is Berkman on Lenin, whose strength he describes as "intellectual, that of the profound conviction of an unimaginative nature"—a mentality not dissimilar to that of Zozulya's Ak:

> The dictatorship of the proletariat is vital, Lenin emphasized. It is the sine qua non of the revolutionary period, and must be furthered by all and every means. To my contention that popular

initiative and active interest are essential to the success of the Revolution, he replied that only the Communist Party could lead Russia out of the chaos of conflicting tendencies and interests. Liberty, he said, is a luxury not to be permitted at the present stage of development. When the Revolution is out of danger, external and domestic, then free speech might be indulged in. The current conception of liberty is a bourgeois prejudice, to say the least. Petty middle-class ideology confuses revolution with liberty; in reality, the Revolution is a matter of securing the supremacy of the proletariat. Its enemies must be crushed, and all power centralized in the Communist State. In this process the Government is often compelled to resort to unpleasant means; but that is the imperative of the situation, from which there can be no shrinking. In the course of time these methods will be abolished, when they have become unnecessary.

In the mid-1930s, living in France under strained circumstances and in failing health, Berkman's mind turned to Zozulya's story once again. He must have felt its message was urgently relevant. He committed suicide on 28 June 1936.

The perils of ideological rigidity and the dehumanizing forces of autocracy were also the central concerns of Yevgeny Zamyatin (1884–1937), whose classic novel We (1919–21)—which has inspired the dystopian visions of Aldous Huxley, George Orwell and countless others—earned the distinction of being the first work officially banned by the Soviet censorship bureau in 1921. Zamyatin was born in Lebedyan, some two hundred miles south of Moscow, to an Orthodox priest father and pianist mother. Never happy in the provinces, he left for St Petersburg in 1902 to receive an education as a navel engineer and soon became involved in radical politics. Not long after joining the Bolshevik Party in 1906 he was arrested and sent back to his home town. He returned to St Petersburg illegally in 1908, left the party and began to write fiction; for the next five years he lived under constant threat of rearrest, until the tsarist authorities granted him and many other internal exiles amnesty in 1913, on the occasion of the tercentenary of Romanov rule. However, the publication of *A Godforsaken Hole* (1913), a novella exposing the dreadful conditions under which soldiers lived in provincial garrisons, led to another arrest and exile to Kem in Northern Russia. In 1916, having served his sentence, Zamyatin was dispatched to Newcastle upon Tyne to oversee the building of icebreakers for the Russian Imperial Navy, returning to Petrograd just in time to witness the October Revolution. As his novella *The Islanders* (1917) shows, he didn't much like life in England, but what he witnessed at home under the Bolsheviks simply appalled him. Aside from *We*, his most powerful and prophetic fictional recastings of Soviet reality are the short story 'The Cave' (1922) and the brief fable 'The Dragon' (1918), in which the titular beast is a Red Army soldier, whose fading humanity is briefly rekindled by the sight of a frozen starling.

Although Zamyatin was a key figure in Gorky's World Literature Publishing House in the early 1920s, translating many important works into Russian, and exerted great influence on the so-called Serapion Brotherhood of younger Soviet writers, who lived and studied at the House of Arts in Petrograd, he soon became something of an internal exile under the Soviets—just as he had been for many years under tsarist rule. He faced severe attacks in the Soviet press after the Russian text of *We* was published in Prague in 1927. In 1931 he brazenly wrote to Stalin, asking to be allowed to emigrate. "To me as a writer," he explained, "being deprived of the opportunity to write is nothing less than a death sentence. Yet the situation that has come about is such that I cannot continue my work, because no creative activity is possible in an atmosphere of systematic persecution that increases in intensity from year to year." Surprisingly—and likely owing to Gorky's intervention—permission was granted, and Zamyatin and his wife left for the West, eventually settling in Paris. Zamyatin was a difficult person, a contrarian under all circumstances; he refused to make inroads in the émigré community. Isolated and crippled by sciatica, he spent the last years of his life writing *The Scourge of God*, a novel set in the time of Attila the Hun. It was never completed. He died of a heart attack on 10 March 1937.

YEFIM ZOZULYA (1891–1941)

The Dictator
The Story of Ak and Humanity

I. THE UNEXPECTED

It seemed a day like any other. The city looked the same as usual. Streets and houses had their ordinary appearance. The sky wore its customary blue. The pavements spread grey and indifferent, as always. Suddenly some men appeared carrying large buckets of paste. They began to put up posters on the walls, doing it quickly, with tears streaming into the buckets. The posters were terse and to the point:

CITIZENS!

THE COUNCIL OF PUBLIC WELFARE has decided to reorganize life on the basis of justice and progress. For this purpose the COUNCIL will pass on the Right to Life of every inhabitant of our city. Those whose existence is found to be superfluous will cease to exist within 24 hours. Appeals against the decisions of the COUNCIL may be filed, in writing, within that time. All appeals will be decided by the COUNCIL before sunset of the same day.

REMARKS:

1. Every inhabitant is to submit to the orders of the COUNCIL OF PUBLIC WELFARE unconditionally and absolutely. A

Committee of the COUNCIL consisting of three members will visit every house. Their questions are to be answered truthfully. Everyone whose existence is found to be superfluous will be examined personally, and a record kept.

2. This order goes into effect with its publication. No unnecessary human material will be tolerated. No sentimental considerations will be allowed to interfere with our plans for the public welfare. This applies to all the inhabitants of our city without exception, including men, women, children, rich and poor.

3. Those who will lack the courage to terminate their existence, if ordered to do so by the COUNCIL OF PUBLIC WELFARE, will be aided by the COUNCIL. The sentences will be carried out by the friends and neighbours of the condemned, or by a special military detachment.

4. No person may leave the city until the work of determining the Right to Life has been completed.

THE COUNCIL OF PUBLIC WELFARE

2. THE CITIZENS

"Have you read it?"

"Seen the posters?"

"Is it possible?"

"Read it?"

People began to collect at every street corner. Soon the crowds grew so large that traffic ground to a halt. Some persons suddenly grew so weak they had to lean against the walls for support. Many wept. Others fainted. By nightfall great numbers of the inhabitants were ill.

"Have you read it?"

"Terrible!"

"Outrageous!"

"It's our own fault! We elected the Council! Why did we give them such power?"

"True! True!"

"It's our own fault!"

"It was a terrible mistake! But who would have believed such a thing! We thought the Council would help bring better times. But—to resort to such methods!"

"Such good men in the Council, too!"

"Indeed, they are! And Ak has been elected President of the Council!"

"What! Really! Why, that's great! Where did you hear it?"

"I'm just coming from the Council headquarters. It's a fact: Ak has been elected all right."

"What luck! Ak's a fine man!"

"Yes, yes! He's a just man!"

"Friends, Ak is the right man. I rejoice to hear that he has become President of the Council. He is a just and wise man."

"True, true! His decisions will be just, I'm sure!"

"Citizens, we need not worry about it. I know Ak—he's all right. We may depend on his good judgement and sense of justice. Only the evil and useless elements will be eliminated—you can absolutely rely on Ak for that!"

"Yes, I'm sure of it! Ak will never permit any injustice."

"Tell me, dear friend, do you think they will pass favourably on my case? You know that I have always been a good citizen. You remember, of course, that I was in that shipwreck where twenty passengers jumped into one lifeboat. Don't you? There were too many for that boat—it would have capsized—it meant the death of all of us. Well, five men had to be sacrificed—to save the other fifteen. I was the first to volunteer! I jumped overboard and—What's the matter? Why do you smile so incredulously? Of course, I'm old and weak now, but at that time I was young and strong; yes, and brave, too! Indeed, I was! Why, don't you remember that shipwreck? All the papers were full of it at the time! The other four men went down, but I was saved. Just luck! What d'you think, friend, will they let me live?"

"And me? How about me? Didn't I give my whole fortune away to the poor? It's a long time ago, but I have all the documents to prove it. Yes, sir, I have!"

"I don't know. Who can tell? It all depends on the viewpoint of the Council!"

"Let me tell you something, my dear fellow citizens: a primitive helpfulness or usefulness to those around you is not enough to justify one's right to life. Else every stupid servant girl could claim that right. That's silly old nonsense! You are terribly old-fashioned, that's what you fellows are! Really reactionaries!"

"Indeed? What, then, makes a human life valuable? Tell me that!"

"Yes, yes! Tell us!"

"Well—I don't know, but—"

"You don't know? Then what the hell are you talking about?"

"Pardon me, but just let me explain—"

"Look! Look! Something has happened! Everyone's running!"

"A riot! Save yourselves!"

"Help! Help!"

"A panic! Oh, my God!"

"Run, fellows! Run! Save yourselves!"

"Halt! Halt!"

"Stand still, men!"

"Order! Quiet! Don't increase the panic!"

"Halt! Halt!"

3. THE FLIGHT

Excitement, shouting and yelling. Everybody running. Red-cheeked youths, mortal fear in their eyes. Clerks, employees of banks and offices. Bridegrooms in starched white shirts. Gentlemen of leisure. Actors, baseball fans, football huskies. Loafers, swindlers, rowdies. Poets, lovers, writers. Broad-shouldered sportsmen. Dowdies. Frequenters of houses of ill fame. Grafters, windbags, long-haired fakes. Melancholics with yearning black eyes. Misers, on their lips a cynical smile. Good-natured simpletons, clever scoundrels. All ran.

And stout, heavy women ran. Tall, skinny women, haughty, oversexed. Wives of fools and wives of bright men. Gossips, cocottes, prostitutes. Faithless women, brainless, envious. Proud geese, their hair dyed. Indifferent females, good women, grisettes, now all with the same expression of terror on their faces.

And old men ran. Cadaverous, knock-kneed, bow-legged. Stout, fine-looking, ugly, misshapen. Landlords, usurers, prison guards. Self-satisfied whorehouse owners, grey-haired lackeys, respectable grandfathers, a lifetime of swindle and deceit back of them. Fat gamblers, their fingers covered with diamonds, big-bellied libertines.

They all ran, crowds, mobs of them. Great masses of rags were wrapped about their bodies and limbs. Steam poured from their mouths. Their shouts and curses bounced off the well-hidden indifference of the abandoned buildings.

Some ran with their possessions. Desperately they clung to the bags, boxes, pillows and bundles in their hands. For dear life they held on to their jewellery, their money, their children. They yelled and screamed, they turned around, wrung their hands, and ran faster.

But they were all forced to return. Armed men shot—fired volleys into them. Attacked them with clubs and guns, and the runaways turned back, leaving many dead and wounded.

In the evening the city assumed its usual appearance again. The inhabitants kept to their houses, most of them in bed. Desperate hope flickered in their hearts.

4. THE PROCEEDINGS WERE SIMPLE

"Your name?"

"Alexander Ross."

"Age?"

"Thirty-nine."

"Profession?"

"Cigarette maker."

"Don't you lie to me!"

"I'm telling you the truth. I've been fourteen years in the trade. I'm a hard-working man, and I support my family—"

"Where's your family?"

"Here. This is my wife, and there is my son."

"Comrade Doctor, examine them."

"Right away."

"Well, Doctor, what do you say?"

"Citizen Ross is anaemic. General condition medium. His wife is subject to headaches and rheumatism. The boy is well."

"All right, Doc. That will do. Citizen Ross, what are your amusements? What do you enjoy in life?"

"I—I enjoy—I enjoy many things—I enjoy—I love my fellow men and I—love life itself."

"Don't be nervous, Citizen Ross. Be more precise. We've no time to waste. Tell us clearly, what do you love in life?"

"I love—well, my son—he plays the violin so beautifully—and I love a good meal—I mean, I'm no glutton, but I enjoy good food and—I love women—I like to watch them on the street—and I love my work—I make five hundred cigarettes an hour—and a good rest after the day's work—and a lot more besides—I love life—"

"Calm yourself, Citizen Ross, stop your whining. What's *your* opinion, Comrade Psychologist?"

"Poor material, Comrade. A miserable, humdrum existence. Semi-phlegmatic, semi-sanguinical. Activity below medium. No hope of improvement. Passivity seventy-five per cent. Still worse in Mrs Ross. The boy is a simpleton, but perhaps—How old is your son, Mr Ross? Stop crying."

"Thirteen, Sir."

"All right, then. Citizen Ross, your son may go on living. We'll postpone his case for five years. As for you—however, that is not within my jurisdiction. It's up to you, Comrade."

"In the name of the COUNCIL OF PUBLIC WELFARE: For the high purpose of clearing life from all superfluous rubbish, from indifferent existences which clog the way of progress, I command you, Citizen Ross, and you, Mrs Ross, to terminate your lives within twenty-four hours. Don't shout! Stop that! Doctor, give the woman something for her nerves. Call the guard! This fellow will hardly manage it himself."

5. THE GREY CABINET

The Grey Cabinet stood in the corridor of the main office of the Council of Public Welfare. In appearance it was just an ordinary, well-made cabinet, with its usual stupidly thoughtful expression.

It was about three feet wide and less than four feet in depth, but it was big enough to serve as the cemetery for a hundred thousand lives.

The Grey Cabinet bore two short inscriptions:

CATALOGUE OF THE SUPERFLUOUS
Character Records

The Catalogue contained several subdivisions, among them the following:

SUBJECT TO IMPRESSIONS, BUT NOT ABLE TO DIFFERENTIATE
MINOR FOLLOWERS
PASSIVE
LACKING CENTRES

The characteristics were brief and concise. Occasionally there were some ironical remarks by the specialists, but in such cases Ak, the President of the Council, never failed to make a marginal note on the document in red pencil, reading: "The superfluous should not be insulted."

We reproduce herewith some specimen records:

Superfluous Number 14741

Physical condition medium. Is in the habit of visiting acquaintances who don't want him and feel no interest in him. In the blossom of youth he seduced some girl and abandoned her. The greatest event in his life was furnishing a home for the woman he married. Weak-headed. When asked to tell the most interesting thing he knows of life, what he has managed to see, he related his visit at the Hotel Ritz in Paris. The simplest of creatures. The lowest of the common sort. A weak heart. Within 24 hours.

Superfluous Number 14623

Physically sound. Mechanic. Not fond of his job. Type of least resistance. Mentality below par. Subject to the primitive disease: fear of life, fear of liberty. On Sundays and holidays stupefies his brain with strong drink. Exerted energy during the Revolution: wore a red tie and kept buying potatoes because of his cowardly fear of hunger. Proud of his proletarian origin. Took no active part in the Revolution. Fond of cream for his coffee. Beats his children. Daily life grey, prosaic. Within 24 hours.

Superfluous Number 15201

Speaks eight languages. Whatever language he uses, his friends are always bored. Has a passion for studying the mechanism of cigarette lighters. Very self-confident. Seems to have acquired his self-assurance from his philological studies. Demands the greatest respect from all who come in contact with him. A windbag. Entirely indifferent to the higher values of life. Is afraid of beggars. Sweetly amiable with people, purely out of innate cowardice. Is fond of killing flies and other insects. Rarely experiences joy. Within 24 hours.

Superfluous Number 4356

Yells at her servant out of sheer boredom. Secretly eats the film off fresh milk and the fatty layer off the soup. Reads cheap romances. Spends whole days lolling about on the couch. Her deepest desire:

to sew a dress with yellow sleeves and jutting sides. For twelve years, she was the object of a talented inventor's affection. She had no idea what he did for a living—thought he was an electrician. She left him and married a leather merchant. Has no children. Is often capricious and cries for no reason. Wakes in the middle of the night, orders the servant to heat up the samovar, drinks tea and eats. Useless creature. Within 24 hours.

6. THE COUNCIL

President Ak and his Council of Public Welfare were assisted in their labours by a large staff of specialists, among whom there were physicians, psychologists, technicians, inspectors, social workers and writers. All of them worked intensively and rapidly. There were days when a couple of specialists sent as many as a hundred persons to their doom. The Grey Cabinet was bursting with records, in which the exactness of the phrases competed with their authors' limitless self-assuredness.

The offices of the Executive Bureau of the Council resembled a veritable beehive. Work continued there from early morning till late at night. Men kept coming and going, issuing orders, signing papers, sending out execution squads. Scores of clerks sat at long tables writing busily, hardly taking time for lunch.

President Ak was at a separate desk, his hard, narrow eyes staring at something apparently visible only to himself, thinking a thought only he understood, which bent his back and turned the hair on his big, stubborn head ever greyer.

Something was building up between him and his servants; something seemed to have risen between his sleepless thought and the blind, thoughtless hands of the executioners.

7. AK'S DOUBTS

One morning the members of the Council of Public Welfare entered Ak's private study to make their daily report. To everybody's surprise Ak was not in his accustomed place. It was very strange, as the President was famed for his extreme punctuality and settled habits of work.

He could not be found. Messengers were sent to every part of the city. The telephones were kept busy. But President Ak could not be found.

Late that afternoon Ak was accidentally discovered in the Grey Cabinet. They found him sitting on the paper graves of the executed, evidently even deeper in thought than usual.

"What does it mean, Comrade President?" his colleagues asked. "What are you doing here?"

"Can't you see—I'm thinking," he replied wearily.

"But why here?"

"It's the best place for it. I am thinking of the executed, and nothing is more productive of thought than the records of their extermination. These documents here are most informative."

Someone gave a short, dry laugh.

"Don't laugh!" Ak upbraided him sternly, shaking a record in his face. "The study of the lives of the murdered has taught me a great deal. Yes, a great deal," he emphasized. "A crucial moment has arrived. I am thinking of new ways of progress. You people have shown that you can glibly prove the superfluity of a human life. Even the stupid among you can readily mouth a few convincing formulae. But I am sitting here and wondering whether our methods are right."

He sighed deeply, then added, speaking very low: "Where is the right way? When I study the living I come to the conclusion that three-quarters of them should be exterminated. But when I study the dead I begin to doubt my judgement and I feel that—wouldn't it have been better to let them live and to—to love and pity them? I don't know myself—I feel it is the conundrum of the human question, yes, the great tragic conundrum of human history."

He grew silent, a distracted look on his face. Digging down into the mountain of death records he began to read one document after another, aghast at the incredible poverty of their contents.

The members of the Council of Public Welfare retired quietly, without a word. In the first place, because they knew it was useless to object to Ak, and in the second place, because they simply didn't dare to do so. They all felt that a crisis had come—that progress would take a new turn. It did not please them at all: everything had been working so smoothly, in an orderly and systematic manner, and now—what was going to happen now?

What would this man, who had lost his mind, and who had unheard-of power over the town, conceive of now?

8. THE CRISIS

President Ak disappeared.

A thorough search was made, but Ak could not be found. Some said he had been seen on the outskirts of the city, sitting in a tree and weeping. Others claimed that Ak had been seen in his garden, crawling on all fours and eating dirt.

The activities of the Council of Public Welfare began to lose their former vim and energy. Somehow things did not work right in the absence of Ak. Presently trouble started. Some citizens barricaded their doors and refused to admit the examiners and specialists of the Council. Others even dared to laugh off the questions about their right to life and to defy the executioners. Soon the situation grew very serious. Cases of disobedience and resistance multiplied. Finally some of the boldest inhabitants decided to arrest the chief dignitaries of the Council and to subject them to the test of superfluity.

Wild excitement reigned in the city. Superfluous citizens, already condemned but not yet executed, began to appear on the streets, contrary to the strict orders of the authorities. It was well known that the appearance of a condemned on the streets was an offence invariably punished by immediate death. Moreover, the condemned behaved with the greatest impudence, as if they had a right to live. They ignored the decisions and commands of the Council and nonchalantly took up their former lives again. They indulged in their customary recreations and some even celebrated marriages. The government and the press declared that it was nothing short of anarchy.

On the streets the people rejoiced. "At last! At last! Hurrah!"

"Hurrah for life!"

"Three cheers for the condemned!"

"Down with the superfluity tests!"

"Down with the Council!"

"Down with the murderers!"

"Don't you think, Citizen, that life has become a bit easier now? There's a good deal less superfluous human junk now. There's more elbow room, so to speak."

"Shame on you! Do you mean that the executed had no right to life? Why, I know a great many that should really be done away with, but they are still among us. Yes, indeed! Let me tell you this, my good man, some of the best and noblest men have been eliminated. Believe me, I know what I am talking about!"

"That may be so, Citizen, but mistakes are liable to happen. By the way, tell me, do you know what has become of Ak?"

"Search me! It's very strange, though!"

"Ak was seen up a tree and weeping all the time."

"Nonsense, man! Ak is crawling on all fours in his garden and eating dirt."

"Is that possible?"

"My wife swears her mother's cousin saw him with her own eyes."

"I don't believe it!"

"Old women's tales!"

"What is it? About Ak?"

"Oh, to hell with Ak!"

"T' hell with him! Serves him right!"

"No more Ak for us!"

"You rejoice too soon, my friends. Ak is to return this evening, and the Council will take up its work in earnest now."

"What? What!"

"Where d'you get that?"

"How do you know? Who told you?"

"Never mind who told me, I know it, all right. There's too much human rubbish left yet, that's what I say! We must get rid of it. We've got to clean our city thoroughly. It's not half done yet!"

"Th' hell you say!"

"Don't you talk to me like that or I'll—"

"Look, look, fellows! They're putting up posters again! There, on the corner!"

"Oh, my God!"

"I'll run over and see!"

"Let's go over and read them, boys!"

"Make way! Make way! The posters!"

"Lord in heaven, have mercy on us!"

"Out of the way, everybody!"

9. NEW POSTERS

Men carrying large buckets of paste ran puffing through the streets. Packets of gigantic pink posters unrolled with a joyous crackle and were stuck to the walls. Their contents were simple and clear:

FELLOW CITIZENS!

It is hereby announced that every inhabitant of our city has been granted the Right to Life. The order goes into effect at once.

The Council of Public Welfare has been abolished and its destructive work suppressed. Its place has been taken by a new Commission to be known as THE CONTROL OF HUMAN HAPPINESS. Citizens, rejoice! You are, each and every one of you, precious beings. Your right to life is self-evident and incontestable, henceforth and for ever. It is your sacred duty to enjoy and be happy.

THE CONTROL OF HUMAN HAPPINESS has appointed special Committees, consisting of three members, with instructions to visit every inhabitant of the city at least once a day. They will respectfully congratulate the citizens on their Right to Life and prepare the Records of Happiness. You are kindly requested to aid the Committees in their study of happiness by giving them the most detailed information. The Records of Happiness will be kept in the Pink Cabinet and preserved for the benefit of future generations.

THE CONTROL OF HUMAN HAPPINESS

10. THE CHANNELS OF LIFE

Gates and doors were thrown open. Windows and balconies came alive. Voices grew merry. There was laughter, song, music. Stout young ladies pounded the piano.

From early morning till late at night gramophones whizzed. Vile old violins, clarinets and trombones helped along. In the evening the men took off their coats, sat on the verandas with their legs spread wide, listening to the radio and belching their profound contentment.

The streets of the city were crowded. Young fellows went joy-riding with their girls in autos, cabs and on motorcycles built for two. No one feared to leave his house or to be seen on the promenade. In the cafés it was almost impossible to find a vacant seat.

But the most rushing business was done by stores where mirrors and looking glasses were sold. The people became obsessed by the passion of watching their reflection. Photographers and portrait painters worked overtime. These portraits were framed and adorned the walls of private flats. A pair of such portraits even resulted in a murder—it was in all the papers. A young man renting a room in a flat demanded that the portraits of his hosts' parents be removed from his walls. The hosts were offended and killed the young man, tossing him out of the fifth-floor window.

Self-admiration and self-esteem grew enormously. Quarrels and fights multiplied. The hot words usually exchanged on such occasions now assumed a peculiar form:

"It sure was a mistake that you were overlooked by the Council of Public Welfare, superfluous junk that you are! Too bad they didn't complete their job!"

"You bet they didn't complete it, or you wouldn't be here now!"

On the whole, however, such little matters did not affect the general tenor of everyday existence.

The inhabitants indulged in more food and drink than before; their mothers, wives and sweethearts prepared a larger stock of preserves, and the demand for warm underwear increased very considerably, because the people were now more careful of their health.

The Committees of the Control of Human Happiness conscientiously visited the inhabitants and questioned everyone about his life, joy and happiness. Many stated that they were getting along very well indeed, and they took great pains to convince the official inquirers how greatly they enjoyed living.

"Look at me," some would exclaim, "making pickles, curing herring—don't I look fine! I'm all right! Yesterday I weighed myself. Gained eight pounds in two weeks! Not bad, eh? Knock wood!"

There were some, however, who complained about comforts and amenities, and lamented that the Council of Public Welfare hadn't done its job.

"Just think of it," a young man protested, "the other day we got into a street car—my wife and I—and not a single seat to be had! Outrageous! We had to stand several minutes. It's evident that the city is still overcrowded! Too much junk left! They should have eliminated it at the right time, that's what I have to say!"

An old gentleman grumbled: "Be sure to note down, Mr Inspector, that neither yesterday nor the day before was I congratulated on the fact of my existence. It's a shame! Such neglect! You don't expect *me* to come to *you* to receive congratulations, do you?!"

11. AND THEN—

At the headquarters of the Control of Human Happiness everyone was feverishly busy. At the long tables the clerks worked like bees.

The Pink Cabinet was bursting with the Records of Happiness. The documents described the lives of the inhabitants in every detail. Birth dates, marriages, christenings, love affairs and adventures—everything was chronicled at length, frankly and truthfully. Many of the Records read like veritable novels. Presently the citizens requested the Control of Human Happiness to publish the Records for general circulation. There was a tremendous popular demand for such reading matter.

President Ak was at his desk, as before. He sat in silence, evidently in deep thought. His back had become more bent, and his hair had turned white.

From time to time he would walk over to the Pink Cabinet and sit down on the Records there, as he had formerly sat in the Grey Cabinet.

One morning Ak jumped out of the Pink Cabinet, shouting: "They must be exterminated! Yes, exterminated! Destroyed! Killed! Killed!"

But then he gazed fixedly at the men writing at the long tables, recording the living with the same zeal they had recorded the dead. With a despairing wave of his hand he turned and rushed out of the office.

Ak disappeared. Disappeared for ever.

Various stories were circulated about his disappearance. Conflicting stories that before long became legends. But Ak was never found.

Ak had killed off many inhabitants of the city. Ak granted the Right to Life to those that had survived. Ak wanted to kill the inhabitants off again.

But the people, among whom there were some good men, some of indifferent quality and some very poor human material—they continue to live to this day as if Ak had never existed and there had never been any perplexing problem about the Right to Life.

1919

(Translated and adapted by Alexander Berkman)

YEVGENY ZAMYATIN (1884–1937)

The Dragon

Gripped with bitter cold, ice-locked, Petersburg burned in delirium. One knew: out there, invisible behind the curtain of fog, the red and yellow columns, spires and hoary gates and fences crept on tiptoe, creaking and shuffling. A fevered, impossible, icy sun hung in the fog—to the left, to the right, above, below—a dove over a house on fire. From the delirium-born, misty world, dragon men dived up into the earthly world, belched fog—heard in the misty world as words, but here becoming nothing—round white puffs of smoke. The dragon men dived up and disappeared again into the fog. And trolleys rushed screeching out of the earthly world into the unknown.

On the trolley platform a dragon with a gun existed briefly, rushing into the unknown. His cap was down over his nose and would have swallowed the dragon's head but for his ears; on the protruding ears the cap had come to rest. His army greatcoat dangled to the floor; the sleeves flapped loosely; the tips of the boots were turned up, empty. And in the dimness of the fog—a hole: the mouth.

This was now in the leaping, rushing world; and here the bitter fog belched out by the dragon was visible and audible: "So I was taking him along, the bastard: an intellectual mug—it turned your stomach just to look at him. And it talks, the scum! Wouldn't you know? It talks!"

"And did you bring him in?"

"I sure did—non-stop to the heavenly kingdom. With the bayonet."

The hole in the fog closed up. There was nothing now but the empty cap, empty boots, an empty army coat. The trolley, gnashing, out of the world.

And suddenly—from the empty sleeves—from out of their depths, a pair of raw, red dragon claws emerged. The empty coat squatted down on the floor, and in the paws there was a tiny, grey, cold lump that had materialized out of the bitterly cold fog.

"Mother in heaven! A baby starling—frozen stiff! Just look at it!"

The dragon pushed back his cap—and in the fog two eyes appeared, two small chinks from the nightmare world into the human.

The dragon blew with all his might into the red paws, and there were clearly words, spoken to the starling—but in the nightmare world they were unheard. The trolley screeched.

"The little bastard: he gave a flutter, didn't he? Not yet? He'll come around, by Go... Just think!"

He blew with all his strength. The gun dropped to the floor. And at that moment ordained by destiny, at a point ordained in space, the starling gave a jerk, another—and fluttered off the dragon's paws into the unknown.

The dragon's fog-belching maw gaped open to his ears. Then slowly the cap slid down over the chinks into the human world and settled back on the protruding ears. The guide to the heavenly kingdom picked up his gun.

The trolley gnashed and screeched and rushed into the unknown, out of the human world.

1918

(Translated by Mirra Ginsburg)

BLUE BANNERS
AND SCARLET SAILS

The names of Mikhail Prishvin (1873–1954), whose evocations of man's life in the Russian countryside won him a place of honour among nature writers, and Alexander Grin (1880–1932), the consummate romantic dreamer and spinner of naively exotic tales, are not often uttered in the same breath. Yet the authors do have something in common: each, in his own way, found—and offered readers—a means of imaginative and spiritual escape from the reality of Soviet life.

Prishvin was born on his family's estate in the village of Khrushchovo, near the city of Yelets, in Central Russia. His father—a rather dissolute merchant—died when he was seven, and he and his four siblings were raised by their mother. As a boy, Prishvin was expelled from the prestigious Yelets High School (a *gymnasium*) for, among other things, impudent behaviour towards his geography teacher, Vasily Rozanov (see pp. 136–37). He was sent to live with his uncle in Tyumen, in western Siberia, where he completed his secondary education in 1893. That same year he enrolled in the Chemistry and Agriculture Department of the Riga Polytechnical Institute, where he became involved in an underground Marxist circle. In 1897 he was arrested for distributing radical literature and sentenced to solitary confinement. After his release, he received permission to study abroad, at the University of Leipzig, where he earned a degree in Agricultural Engineering in 1902. In Europe Prishvin fell deeply in love with a fellow student. The young woman did not reciprocate his feelings, and the trauma of this rejection proved to be a lifelong inspiration. Much of Prishvin's mature work—especially his novels *Kashchei's Chain* (1927) and *Jen Sheng* (1933)—deals with man's need to overcome a sense of isolation and restore inner balance, often by re-establishing a harmonious relationship with nature.

Prishvin worked as an agronomist in rural Russia until 1905, then decided to devote himself to literature. He first attained success as a lyrical ethnographer of remote Russian lands, but he soon moved towards a more experimental and philosophical mode in his writing; he also drifted away from his socialist convictions, joining the spiritual seekers of the Religious-Philosophical Society, which had been co-founded by his former teacher Rozanov. He appears to have been suspicious of the Bolshevik revolution from the start, withdrawing from Petersburg and Moscow—first to Yelets, and then to the village of Alexino, near Smolensk. Alexino was the home of his wife, Yefrosinia, with whom he had lived since 1903, raising two sons of their own, as well as her son from a previous union. The 1920s, a period of intense societal transformation and literary ferment, were a particularly trying time for the essentially apolitical Prishvin. In 1926 he and his family settled in Sergiyev Posad, where Rozanov had died in 1919, and lived in near-poverty. He found some support in the camp of the "fellow travellers"—authors unaffiliated with, but not hostile to the party—and joined the group Mountain Pass (*Pereval*), which was founded by the influential literary critic Alexander Voronsky (1884–1937), a Marxist humanist and Trotskyist who fell from favour after Stalin's ascent to power and was eventually executed.

As usual, Prishvin sought refuge in nature, and though his writings on the subject were attacked in the 1920s for their irrelevance to Soviet life, they won him a wide readership. Ironically, it may have been the resolute apoliticism of this work that ensured Prishvin's safety in the 1930s, when so many true believers of the previous decade were repressed for having espoused positions that were suddenly deemed heretical. His novel *Jen Sheng* became an international success, and *Nature's Diary* (1925, pub. 1935), a rich chronicle of the cycles of plant and animal life, is a classic of its genre. In his preface to a 1987 English translation of the latter, John Updike praises the evocative power of Prishvin's prose: "The vibration of our animal existence is in him, as well as those tentative motions of mind whereby Man began to subdue his magnificent, riddle-filled environment."

By the end of the 1930s Prishvin was living in comfort in a luxury flat in Moscow. But his remaining years were not free of turmoil. In 1940 he divorced his wife and married his secretary, causing a minor scandal, and his final novel, *The Sovereign's Road* (1949), was kept from publication because of its implicit critique of the consequences of forced progress. Prishvin died of cancer in Moscow on 16 January 1954. Decades later, in the final days of the Soviet era, Prishvin's private diaries were finally released in full. They express his clear and passionate antipathy towards the regime, and especially his resentment of its inhumane, ecologically devastating programmes of industrialization and agricultural collectivization. But Prishvin's published writings of 1917 and 1918 speak just as clearly of his early distaste for the Bolsheviks and their policies. In 'The Blue Banner' the author dramatizes his unwillingness to endorse either side in the bloody conflict unfolding throughout the country; the story was published on 28 January 1918, the day that Alexander Blok completed *The Twelve* (see pp. 50–63), and can be read as a tragic counterpoint to that poem.

While the hero of Prishvin's story marches under a blue banner, recoiling in horror from the blood-red flag of the Bolsheviks, Alexander Grin, Russia's most beloved fantasist, fled the inhospitable climes of the early Soviet era into a land of his own imagining, the subcontinent of Grinlandia, hoisting scarlet sails. Grin was born Alexander Grinevsky in the town of Slobodskoy, near Vyatka (now Kirov), in Russia's Volga region. He was one of five children, and after Grin's mother died of tuberculosis in 1893, his father, an accountant, married another woman, who had a child of her own from a previous marriage. Life in the crowded house was difficult for Grin, and the schools in Vyatka did not inspire him. Like Prishvin, he was expelled for bad behaviour. He found solace in the works of James Fenimore Cooper, Robert Louis Stevenson and Thomas Mayne Reid ("Captain Reid"), an Irishman whose swashbuckling tales of adventure in the American West captivated several generations of young boys in Russia and the Soviet Union. In 1896, eager for adventures of his own, Grin decided to run away to Odessa. Over the following decade, Grin tramped across the empire from Baku to the Urals, working odd jobs (including stints as a lumberjack and miner), enlisting in and promptly deserting the army, and joining the Socialist Revolutionary Party. In 1903 he was arrested for distributing SR propaganda; freed two years later under the amnesty granted in the aftermath of the revolution of 1905, he was rearrested in 1906, only to escape that same year and settle in Moscow.

He made his literary debut in 1906, and adopted his pseudonym in 1907. His early stories are realistic, drawing on his experiences in the political underground, which he clearly found thrilling. But he soon began crafting fiction of a more fantastic hue, modelled on his childhood reading and set on chimerical islands. He was arrested once more in 1910, for having escaped in 1906, and spent two years in exile in the Arkhangelsk Province with his new bride. He took pleasure in the wilderness and seclusion of the far north and, at the same time, lost whatever faith he had left in the revolutionary movement. Returning to St Petersburg in 1912, Grin resumed an active literary and social life; it appears this life put a major strain on his marriage, which ended in 1920. Grin was exhilarated by the events of February 1917 and stayed in Soviet Russia after the Bolshevik revolution. He was drafted into the Red Army in 1919, and served a year until being hospitalized with typhus, from which he barely recovered. It was during his stint with the Bolshevik forces that he completed the work for which he is best remembered, the romantic "fairy tale" *Scarlet Sails* (1923)—a parable of the power of faith and imagination. The stories and novels that followed developed Grinlandia's geography but hewed close to the spirit of the *Sails*. Grin's works were a popular success but, like Prishvin's nature writing, came under attack from dogmatic Soviet critics, who argued that his visions of improbable ports were merely a distraction from the pressing concerns of the day.

Grin drifted away from the centres of political power and the literary establishment. In 1924 he and his second wife, whom he had married in 1921, moved to Crimea—perhaps Soviet Russia's nearest equivalent to Grinlandia. He continued to write but, by 1930, was virtually banned from print. He died of cancer on 8 July 1932. His immediate posthumous fate was no kinder: in the 1940s, during the last years of Stalin's regime, Grin's distinctly non-Soviet fantasies became a target of the so-called "anti-cosmopolitan" campaign and were purged from libraries. It wasn't until 1956—the height of the post-Stalin "Thaw"—that Grin's works were republished, capturing a wider and more devoted audience than they had ever enjoyed during the author's lifetime.

Grin has had his advocates in the West, but it is safe to say that his naive and somewhat clumsy fantasies will never mean as much to anyone as they did to generations of Soviet children and adolescents. No matter how drab and circumscribed their lives might have been, young Soviet readers could always stow away in Grin's pages and sail off to faraway lands, where good inevitably triumphed over evil and faith was always rewarded.

'The Soul's Pendulum', translated here from the manuscript version, was written in the autumn of 1917 and printed in the December of that year by the weekly non-Marxist journal *The Republican*, in a highly redacted form. The story doesn't speak so much to Grin's enthusiasm for the revolution as it does to his conviction that it is a great historical moment, a thrilling adventure that demands one's active participation. The editors of *The Republican* gave the story a very different tone, removing the epithet "great" from "revolution", and cutting the final lines—in which we are told that the disenchanted Repyev has shot himself, that the narrator does not pity this mere "spectator" of life and that he looks forward to a "brightly lit future". Considering what the future held for Grin, one doubts that he would have wished to restore these lines, for all his innate optimism.

MIKHAIL PRISHVIN (1873–1954)

The Blue Banner

I

Us and Semyon Ivanych, it used to be our favourite thing was chasing after tops down at the ironware row of market stalls. Clean off the ice, whittle up a top, then whip it around real good with cow tails. For Semyon Ivanych, the best-loved part was warming up, and for us little ones, it was the amusement. We're chasing that top around and old uncle Mitrofan Sergeyevich, he's right there tightening his sash around his belly, hiding his big beard behind his collar, and he spits, spits into his hand to get ready and he's warming up, too; there's the Kozhukhov brothers' stall next to our uncle's stall, then there's the Yershovs and the Abramovs and company: everybody knows each other and everybody's considered kin somehow, and in the winter everybody's chasing after tops with switches made of cow tails.

Where'd that all go! There's maybe one in ten stalls left in one piece at the ironware row, and now it's only the Cheryomukhins that's left in fish, and they don't even trade in fresh caviar and sterlet—they're on plain old salted wild carp. Compared to the others, things weren't so bad for Semyon Ivanych; the others worked in what came natural to their families: the ones trading in cheap tobacco died with cheap tobacco, the ones in the flour section came to a halt along with the windmills, but Semyon Ivanych, he kept running from one thing to another, just like a little Yid, and he only came to grief in the very last few days, when there were no goods left at all. A rumour went around that maybe the Germans had brought lots of their cheap goods into Petersburg, but Semyon Ivanych couldn't bring himself to head into that hellish pit for cheap German goods—he'd even banished the very thought as indecent. So he didn't go off to Petersburg just for his own gain: it was completely unexpected and he was beside himself, too, as it were; he was going to Lebedyan for a funeral, but landed himself in Petersburg for the cheap German goods.

As it happened, his niece Sonechka passed away during the Nativity Fast—unforeseen, like the telegram said. Semyon Ivanych had known this Sonechka as a little girl about fifteen years ago; he'd loved playing with her and he called her the Kid Goat. He hadn't seen her since then; he'd only heard rumours his Kid Goat was mixed up with actors now and had even gone off to Paris to dance. The way the rails are these days, it's hard to say why Semyon Ivanych took it into his head to go off to some half-forgotten relative's funeral; either he had nothing better to do and something strange had started brewing in his person (we'd always considered Semyon Ivanych a little strange), or maybe it's that his family was in a bad way (the eldest boy had taken to theft), or maybe it's this ruin all over the place that made the old ways unfurl like a blue banner, flying in the face of everything new, everything red, that made him want to pay back, in the old way, the ancient way, his kinship debt to the little Kid Goat, daughter of his unlucky brother who'd gone bust trading in Livny accordions. Whatever the case, Semyon Ivanych got ready fast and left for the funeral.

At the junction station where some trains go in the Petersburg direction and others to Lebedyan, a Lebedyan midwife he knew got off her train during the stop and boom—she tells him about Sonechka, that his Kid Goat'd done herself in, a shot to the heart.

There were three things Semyon Ivanych feared on this earth: the first was mountain drop-offs, something he, a steppe-dweller, had never seen but dreamt of often—he'd see himself walking up to a drop-off and the drop-off's tugging at him. He had a second fear, of magicians, that if the magicians or mesmerists did not, indeed, turn out to be the deceivers everybody said they were, and they really could do all that—well, then, it's enough to make you lose your mind: pretty scary! And the third was suicide; the thought of that tugs at you just like the drop-off, and there's only one means of salvation: run away without even thinking, as if it were a drop-off.

Semyon Ivanych found himself a place to sit at the station's little gatehouse, laid his hands on his tummy, and twiddled his thumbs as if they were a windmill: you see this all the time in merchant life, where they'll twiddle their thumbs all around and around for an hour, two hours, however long it takes, until everything's been run through the mill and a new decision comes out.

So imagine: there'd been this clear and forthright person, he'd traded, warmed up, chased after tops with cow tails, and everybody knew his value, and they took stock in what he said, and paid him due respects, too—and just you try and recognize him at that junction station, all alone, sitting for hours, twiddling his thumbs and cranking out something utterly senseless: he'd intended on going to a funeral but found out the deceased had done herself in, so he went to Petersburg for cheap German goods.

II

Semyon Ivanych arrived in Petersburg all right, but getting out proved harder: he ordered a ticket and they promised it by 15 December, so you just sit there a whole week, with nothing to do in that pit of hell. It ended up there weren't any cheap German goods, just all kinds of nonsense: bits of flint, lighters, a little cocoa—and the prices they were asking! There isn't a thing for a merchant to do. Wine cellars being looted, shooting everywhere, and the people's faces—enough to give you a fright. Things are still more or less all right during the day—but at night Semyon Ivanych's fears come together in his room, worse than any nightmare or premonition.

"Suppose," he thinks to himself, "it isn't our Russian people that's doing all this, but magicians and mesmerists."

And then Semyon Ivanych's ancient fear of magicians whispers something else: "And what if it's all the real truth, and this is the life we get all the way till the second coming?"

His second fear, the one about the drop-off, tortures him all the time in his room, too: it's all bright and warm, but then suddenly the electric light goes out with no warning at all, and you're sitting there with a thin little wax candle, just like you're over a drop-off.

And then the third fear sneaks up, the suicide fear, and you might as well go out to the pitch-black street, unbutton your hairy chest, and say, "Gun me down, lads—it's all the same in the end!"

But God forbid he go outside: soon as dusk starts falling, there goes Semyon Ivanych, run-run-running to his room, and he circles around there like a hare, all alone with his fears on a barren island with the water rising.

On the morning of the 15th, a boy brought a ticket for a train at ten in the evening. Semyon Ivanych rejoiced, left for the railway station before nightfall to economize on the tram, and put the crate of tea he'd bought at his feet, nice and careful, so it wasn't bothering anybody. For ten roubles, a soldier got him a window seat in first class—and a good, honest soldier he was, too: he held on to the crate of tea for him, used it as his seat in the lavatory.

Semyon Ivanych settled in and crossed himself: "Bring me home, Lord!"

Suddenly, at around ten in the evening, they announce: "The train's not leaving!" A blizzard was raging. Sundered Rus was snowed under, yoked into one white and boundless kingdom, just like before.

On the return tram, the number five, from Znamenskaya Square to Vasilyevsky Island, Semyon Ivanych once again put the crate of tea at his feet, nice and careful, not bothering anybody. He could hear machine guns shooting, but that wasn't scary on the tram, around people. After crossing Nikolaevsky Bridge, the number five suddenly stopped and the light shut off in the tram; and the number eighteen, which was running right behind the five, shut off, too; and all the trams in the capital, wherever they were running, stopped on the spot and their lights shut off: there was no current. They waited an hour, two—who wants to walk in a blizzard when there's shooting?! But it couldn't be helped, so the passengers scattered, disappearing one after another into the blizzard; and then, finally, the conductor left.

Semyon Ivanych with his heavy crate—fifty pounds of tea, all told—is the last to leave, and he looks around: there's no light, not even a flicker around him, and not one single person anywhere, and it seems that if someone were to appear, he'd be scarier than the fiercest beast. But lots of people would be fine. Hoping to find lots of people on Bolshoy Avenue, Semyon Ivanych hurries off like he's being chased; he's running for all he's worth, gasping for breath under the weight of the crate. It's even worse on Bolshoy Avenue, though—empty as a Siberian wasteland, even emptier: it's been that way in Siberia since the beginning of time, but here you've got an avenue and huge buildings—and nobody, not a soul!

The wind carries the sound of rapid shooting from the harbour, and it seems so close that you think you'll be left here for good, in this foreign land. And then Semyon Ivanych's Kid Goat, the deceased—his niece Sonechka—appeared plainly before him, all snow-white, and she's whimpering, asking: Why did he abandon her in Lebedyan, why did he trade in her little funeral for one so big, and no less unrighteous? The apparition wavered and flew off, and a huge grey monster appeared in the blizzard: crouching, growing, crouching, growing and waving, waving right at Semyon Ivanych.

He dropped the crate, stepped aside, crossed himself, and the huge thing hurtling out of the blizzard right at Semyon Ivanych turned out to be a little black dog.

Then three mountains emerged and walked up to Semyon Ivanych in the form of three civilians with rifles. They inspected the top of the crate and broke it open: tea!

"Marauder!"

And they led Semyon Ivanych off somewhere.

III

In a room once graced by daydreaming noble maidens, whose names were registered in a velvet book, sit two generals playing checkers; a third general is sweeping the room. New detainees are brought in every hour. Two polished little old men—they were directors of departments once—try to go to sleep but can't; they leap up from any noise, realize where they are, and lie down again, then leap up again like wind-up toys. A colonel, an elderly man with a Cross of St George on his chest, keeps muttering something about Metropolitan Antony. At midnight someone in the hallway shouts, "Caught a marauder!"

And they bring in Semyon Ivanych. This bulky, dishevelled, snow-covered man, with streaks of grey in his black hair, casts his fiery eyes around the room and sits down heavily on a stool.

Semyon Ivanych's hands are on his tummy, his thumbs tirelessly twiddling, one around the other, for one hour, two hours. The barmy colonel with the Cross of St George keeps telling him, like a friend, about his plans for the motherland's salvation: first thing tomorrow he's filing a petition with Metropolitan Antony, asking permission to go to all the hooligans' dens and hideouts and gather those roughnecks under Christ's blue banner.

"They've been led astray," he said, "but our roughnecks are godly people, I tell you!"

Semyon Ivanych is listening to the colonel carefully, but he's looking sideways at the generals playing checkers, noticing how a piece is getting forced into a dead end, getting blocked.

"The people were led astray," the colonel keeps muttering.

"That's it, blocked!" announces the general.

Then Semyon Ivanych mumbles something, gladdening the colonel very much: he'd found his voice after all.

"I," says he, "will gather all the roughnecks for the metropolitan, gather them under the blue banner, and bring them all to the metropolitan for a benediction, and Russia will be saved."

Night deepens. Where the Smolny's noble maidens, registered in the velvet book, once took their rest, now sleeps a heap of arrested generals, and a former member of the State Duma, and a member of the Constituent Assembly, and all kinds of socialists and bureaucrats—and it's only Semyon Ivanych that's awake, just twiddling his thumbs.

The Smolny Sweet Reverie makes her way through the corridors and archways into the hall with the double-height ceiling, where, as a princess, Catherine the Great danced with the last Polish king, and then she vanishes in the upper windows, which are turning a lighter blue.

The morning turns lighter, bluer. The prisoners wake up one after another, and they're all watching Semyon Ivanych: he's sitting on that same stool, just like before, and twiddling his thumbs—hasn't stirred since yesterday. The fussy general's getting ready for tea, and the department directors, socialists and deputies are getting up to relieve themselves.

The clock strikes ten, eleven, twelve... At one, they come for Semyon Ivanych: "Questioning!"

Well, Semyon Ivanych had thought he'd be brought in for questioning, and there'd be judges sitting there—my, was he surprised: he'd seen these people before, they were familiar—oh, how familiar—he'd lived his whole life with them, these very ones, and here they were, in the afterlife.

"Hello, friends of mine!"

The sullen judges don't say a word.

"Getting mighty full of yourselves, are you? Come on, you devils—don't you recognize me?"

And he laughs—oh, does he laugh.

They ordered Semyon Ivanych be led out, but as he left, he managed to slip in, "Ah, you roughnecks, you—how godly you are!"

During his night in confinement some kind of secret was revealed to Semyon Ivanych, which had made sense of this whole mess, and all his fears fell away, as if he had outrun them, and had himself become a fright. And now he marches off into the very blaze, into the thick of it, where there's no turning back, to the wine cellars, where the Red Guards are shooting off the drunkards for the third day straight. Semyon Ivanych marches, marches right through the bullets to get to the drunkards, no fear at all.

"Cheers, lads!"

"Our Excellency!" answer the drunkards.

A red-headed, tousled, thoroughly drunk little soldier brings over some wine.

"Under the blue banner, forward march!" commands Semyon Ivanych.

"Right!" answers the redhead.

The madmen and the drunkards set out into the hail of bullets, and the bullets don't graze them: madmen and drunkards have no fear, they themselves are a fright. Sledges, trucks and automobiles move aside, trams stop to let the madman through with his troops.

And that's how it seems to Semyon Ivanych—that it isn't one drunkard drifting behind him, but all the regiments, the whole of drunken Rus marching under the blue banner. Now Semyon Ivanych doesn't fear a thing: Semyon Ivanych himself is a fright. Passers-by stand aside in horror, ordinary people watch from afar as they parade: the madman in front, the drunkard in the back, in strange, deceptive agreement.

1918

(Translated by Lisa Hayden)

ALEXANDER GRIN (1880–1932)

The Soul's Pendulum

Spectacular tragedies burst into bloom against the background of the unreality in which we find ourselves.

Most of them are tragedies of love, of death, of heroism, of an overwrought mind and of a descent into viciousness.

But there are tragedies that flower like rare orchids amid all those black roses and stiff immortelles. I came across one such tragedy.

Picture a man of thirty, sickly-looking, but with a calm expression on his face, seated by an open window. The man is clad in a housecoat and street shoes. On his head is a light-blue skullcap, either Tartar or Greek in origin. On the window sill before him are a glass of strong tea, blackcurrants, cigarettes and an open book—the fifth volume of Count Eugène Salias's collected works.

His young grey cat sits across from him with a light-blue ribbon around her neck, licking herself clean.

From the very start of our meeting, I was struck by the fact that this man, my host, seemed to listen very closely to my reports—my tales of military and revolutionary events—but limited his responses to a curt nod at best. For the most part, he simply popped blackcurrants into his mouth with great relish, or sat still and smoked. At last, my tales were done.

Repyev stayed silent for a while, and then said, somewhat abstractedly:

"Yes. All kinds of things happen in this world of ours."

With unconcealed surprise, I asked him:

"You aren't interested in what's happening now?"

"I am… in a way," he replied listlessly and turned his attention back to the plate of currants.

"I just don't recognize you," I continued. "Barely a year ago, you couldn't sleep at night—you talked until you were hoarse about events that were considerably less interesting than the present round of upheavals. You jumped at the creak of a door. Newspapers were your daily sustenance. You belonged to that camp of our contemporaries who felt that *this* reality was pummelling their brains and crushing their souls. I can see that these here are your volume of Count Salias and your cat, this is your river view and these are your blackcurrants, but *you*, I can't see *you* in this man sitting before me, patiently picking out spoilt berries and arranging them into a neat round pile."

Repyev brightened. It seemed that I had touched upon an issue that was of interest to him.

"Yes, that I know," he began with a smile. "But here's what I'd like you to tell me: Have you ever experienced the feeling of *historical* envy?"

I confessed that I didn't understand him.

"I probably chose the wrong term," Repyev continued. "I'll explain what I mean. When we look back at the past, at certain astonishing pages of history, filled with events, words and acts of fabulous grandeur, with figures great and terrible, with tragic tableaux and dramas of individual lives, as varied as multi-coloured fireworks, when all of this resounds within us like a melody, a melody as complex as the sensation of being in love, a melody refined by centuries of art that resorted to brush and chisel, quill and piano key, to immortalize poetically what has taken place, we—or I, in any case—always feel a feverish yearning to live in those epochs, to take part in those events…"

"Or in similar events," I interrupted him.

"Or in similar events, yes. I'd have settled for being your average man on the street, as long as I could be a contemporary of those exhilarating and magnificent upheavals. Even history's victims seemed to me to be Fate's chosen ones, who wept with joy at their lot."

"That's a common optical illusion."

"Yes. But back then, before the war... You know how grey and nondescript my life was back then, the life of a little pencil pusher... That was before I understood the deeper meaning of that eleven-letter word: 'perspective'. Take, for example, a painting that depicts a landscape, and compare it to a depiction of history. Just as you could never actually walk into the background of a painted perspective in order better to discern what you think is depicted there—the type of mountain, forest, and so on—you could never hope to penetrate history's perspective in order to find out how the masses really lived in those days; the masses are just the background and backdrop of history's depictions... In the background everything is murky, blurred and sketchy. It's only in the foreground that bright personalities emerge, along with scenes of heroic struggles... Meanwhile, back in 1914, I myself was living in the background of a historical perspective... At the time, of course, I couldn't perceive my life as being a part of a perspective or of anything else, but experienced it simply as myself going through whatever I was going through.

"But then the war broke out, and then came the thunder of the Great Revolution. I concede that there had never been *such* a war before. I also concede that the scale of our revolution dwarfs the Great French Revolution like some monstrous giant. However, the first set of upheavals, which dragged on and turned chronic, wore me out in four years' time, just as the water barrel wears out the nag that pulls it, while the changeover of countless indisputably historical personages upon their outsized pedestals—large and extra-large—became an everyday affair. I expected to fall in love with that historical moment and to experience the joy of the magician who enters palaces and temples with the help of a magic poppy seed. But instead I clearly saw who had holes in his boots, who was taking sedative drops, and who went where to buy his butter. I saw that it was raining, that the yard-keepers were sweeping the pavements and that a man's legs grew weary from walking just as they had in the times of Caesar and Marat. I got used to gunshots, I can now coolly discuss hunger strikes, and were a Zeppelin's bomb to blast away half a city, it would cause me only the mildest of shocks. And I became *just* as bored with it all as I had been before the war, when police officers dozed in the sunshine, when the fireman's casque rested in the middle of the kitchen table, when Nekrasov's poems were sung during May Day rallies by amorous school children. I finally understood that a Parisian living in 1793 had every right to pass by a guillotine distractedly, as indifferent to the sound of the blade as to the tic-toc of a clock.

"Here's what happened next. The year 1913 itself moved into the distant perspective and I found myself looking back with trepidation and envy upon its fragrant, calm summer, its lazy winter, its groaning tea-time tables, its cold vodka, its books about love and its complacent thoughts about 'this and that, and nothing else besides…'. How happy were the people who… (See above.) I came here riding upon the train roof, genuinely moved by the thought that soon I'd be eating fried river perch and going mushroom-hunting… Only recently my soul had been trumpeting for an uprising, but now it is just as elated to echo the buzzing of the mosquitoes."

"And then?"

"Give it time. At some point, stuffed to the gills with all this—don't laugh!—historical well-being, I will again utter those fateful words…"

"You mean, 'See above?'"

"Yes. Weren't they fortunate! Marat! Napoleon! The Red and White Roses! Mary Stuart! Spartacus! Carthage! Rome!"

"Excellent. Ho-ho-ho!"

"Forty men on a dead man's chest. Yo-ho-ho and a bottle of rum."

A week later, I was told that Repyev had shot himself.

I did not feel sorry for him. He had chosen the spectator's path.

Meanwhile, awe-inspiring life was blazing all around and merging its heroic melody with the elated voices of the soul, hearkening to the brightly lit future.

1917

(Translated by Maria Bloshteyn)

FUTURE PROSPECTS

O f all the authors featured in this collection, Mikhail Bulgakov (1891–1940) needs least introduction. His masterpiece *The Master and Margarita*—written between 1928 and 1940 but not published until the 1960s—is a classic of twentieth-century world literature, probing the fundamental questions of human dignity and the autonomy of art, and anticipating the techniques of Latin American "magic realism" by some two decades. Born into a religious and intellectual family in Kiev, Bulgakov was educated at an elite secondary school and then studied medicine at Kiev University, from which he graduated in 1916. His studies were temporarily interrupted by bad health and the outbreak of the First World War. He volunteered as a medic. After a few months at the front, he was assigned to a village hospital in the Smolensk Province, and his experiences there form the basis of *A Young Doctor's Notebook* (1925–26). In 1917, he began using morphine to counter the pain associated with diphtheria anti-toxins and briefly became addicted, abandoning the drug for good in 1918.

Bulgakov returned to Kiev on the cusp of civil war. He was drafted as a medic into the Ukrainian People's Army and, shortly thereafter, into the Armed Forces of South Russia—which put him squarely on the side of the Whites. On a sleepless night in the autumn of 1919, while serving with a Cossack regiment in the North Caucasus, Bulgakov was moved to write down his thoughts about Russia's fate. He submitted the piece to a local newspaper, which published it in late November. 'Future Prospects'—a Jeremiad from a broken-down train—was Bulgakov's literary debut.

In 1921, instead of emigrating after the Whites' defeat, Bulgakov moved to Moscow and launched a career as a Soviet author. Many of his works from the 1920s—especially the novel *The White Guard* (1922–1925, but not published in full until 1966) and the plays *Days of the Turbins* (1925, adapted from *The White Guard*) and *Flight* (1927)— look back on the revolution and the Civil War, offering daringly complex, humanizing portraits of the Whites without taking an overtly anti-Soviet stance. Carefully, at times faltering and enduring attacks, Bulgakov negotiated a place for himself in the Soviet literary establishment without compromising his integrity. Stalin acknowledged that the author was "not one of us", but personally adored *Days of the Turbins* and ensured that it was staged repeatedly at the Moscow Art Theatre throughout the 1930s. But bold as Bulgakov was, never again did he allow himself to speak as freely in print as he had in 1919. It is telling that the author pasted the clipping of 'Future Prospects' into his album face-down—a memento for himself, and a message precariously preserved for readers of later generations.

The botched literary debut of satirist Mikhail Zoshchenko (1894–1958) also lay buried for years. Translator Rose France writes:

'A Wonderful Audacity' was written in 1918 under the pseudonym "M.M. Chirkov". In March of that year, Mikhail Zoshchenko (already invalided out of the tsarist army after having been gassed) had returned to Petrograd from Arkhangelsk, where he had been stationed under Kerensky's government as adjutant to the commander of the Arkhangelsk Voluntary Guard when the Bolsheviks took power in the capital. This piece was, probably mistakenly, identified by Zoshchenko's wife Vera as having been rejected in no uncertain terms by the paper *Krasnaya gazeta* (*The Red Gazette*), with the comment: "We need rye bread, not brie cheese." The rejection probably relates to another "mannered" work of the period, but it clearly made a deep impression on Zoshchenko, who later recounted the episode in his autobiography, *Before Sunrise*. 'A Wonderful Audacity' was rejected around the same time as the story mentioned, but, for obvious reasons, Zoshchenko avoided drawing attention to its existence.

The sketch differs markedly from Zoshchenko's mature literary work. Here, the reader senses the influence of Nietzschean thought and mannerisms, which were so popular at the turn of the century. The tone is portentous; the populist "philistine" narrative mask that brought Zoshchenko such success as a satirist in the 1920s has not yet attached itself firmly to the writer's face. But for all this, there is a philosophical continuity between 'A Wonderful Audacity' and Zoshchenko's later writing. Certain themes explored here resurface throughout his work: the love triangle in which animal passion plays a decisive role (here used symbolically, as an expression of the *zeitgeist* in between the revolutions); and the opposing extremes of decadence and lifelessness and barbarism (an idea that later became linked with Zoshchenko's obsession with physical and psychological health).

Ambivalence is integral to Zoshchenko's literary manner. His works often resist conclusive interpretation, and as a result he had the rare ability to find an audience on both sides of the political divide. While a household name in the Soviet Union, he was also read by White émigrés in Western Europe. 'A Wonderful Audacity' can be read either as a genuine paean to brute force, or as a warning about the violence and terror unleashed on the country due to popular desire for a strong hand. Where exactly Zoshchenko stood vis-à-vis the Bolsheviks is not entirely clear, but he remained in Russia and on the side of the "people" in the Civil War. Not only did he reject an offer to emigrate to France in March 1918, in June of that year he manned a telephone post for the Red Army's border defence. Zoshchenko's wife was later to comment that 'A Wonderful Audacity' was one of "only two pieces (which) actually give an impression of the time in which they were written". The other is a feuilleton written in June 1918, 'I Do Not Like You At All, My Lord and Master'—perhaps the most unequivocally anti-Bolshevik piece Zoshchenko ever wrote. It is told from the point of view of a quietly resistant "fellow traveller" and draws an acerbic portrait of one of the self-important victors of the new order, in "his nice new greatcoat" and with his illiterate and empty speech mannerisms: "Today I'll instigate the question for said purposes." It ends with the narrator saying loudly after him as he leaves: "I do not like you at all, my lord and master." The narrator here may bear some resemblance to Zoshchenko himself, and yet cannot be totally identified with him; nor does he come out particularly well from the piece, as he is characterized by a certain faint-heartedness ("And because my face was kind and sympathetic, and because the slight sneer on my lips was hidden by my moustache, he sensed a liking for him"). Here, in the more realistic form of a short exchange, we see again the opposition between spinelessness and brute force, and there is no doubt which of the two will triumph.

Like Bulgakov, Zoshchenko managed to negotiate the turbid and dangerous waters of the Soviet literary scene throughout the 1920s and 1930s. Unlike Bulgakov, who died of natural causes in 1940, Zoshchenko became the target of a new campaign of persecution after the Second World War. This attack on work that was "formalist"—that is, the least bit complex—or "individualistic" was led by Andrey Zhdanov (1896–1948), whom Stalin had appointed to direct the Soviet Union's cultural policy in 1946. Its primary targets were Zoshchenko, the poet Anna Akhmatova (see pp. 26–27) and the composers Sergey Prokofiev (1891–1953) and Dmitry Shostakovich (1906–75). Zoshchenko was ostracized, deprived of work and reduced to poverty for the last decade of his life.

MIKHAIL ZOSHCHENKO (1894–1958)

A Wonderful Audacity

History loves adventurers and speaks of them often, sometimes more than it speaks of men of genius.

Now I leaf through the old, faded pages of the chapters of our recent past.

There is much, much that is sad here, still more that is long dead, and still more, look: pages and pages—on Kerensky...

Do you remember how all Petersburg whispered, smirking and choking on its own laughter, that Kerensky was feeble, that it was disagreeable to feel his feeble hands upon us, that there were many words, an abyss of words, but no bold audacity, none of the audacity of the lord and master, no creative audacity, no ruthlessness towards one's enemies. There was none of this. And how could there be, if a lord and master begins at just that point where Kerensky ends?

Kerensky... His soul, like a little painted courtesan. We remember well his finely turned-out phrases, clipped, abrupt and often strident, they sank into the air more often than they sank into our hearts.

And we still remember the lesson Kerensky taught us—the lesson of feeble politics. His feeble hands committed more crimes than they did good deeds.

And now, when so much has already happened, those far-off days seem to us dull, obscure, verbose.

How much he loved to talk, our feeble lord and master!

But recalling this now, we can only smile, quietly, thoughtfully, and talk in whispers, as though we were talking of some shades or ghosts who had already passed over into an unknown kingdom.

And now here are the most recent days in our history.

I don't remember if it was Kuprin or Tan who, in a moment of high-flown rapture, declared that the power of the Bolsheviks appealed to him, that he felt that here was a strong power, a power just as it should be—a strong power, ruthless towards its enemies.

He spoke sincerely and, it seemed, with some amazement. And I remember how for some time afterwards the bourgeois whispered, absorbing this felicitous notion, and how—also, apparently in amazement—it shrugged its shoulders and chewed at the words with its discontented, fastidious lips: "Oh, the Bolsheviks are standing strong. Very strong. That's not Kerensky for you."

Oh, yes, a great many people went about bent-backed and discontented, and they too growled: "Oh, yes—the devil knows they're strong!"

And it was true—they were strong, and bold, and even audacious.

Audacious in the face of the whole world.

It's true, I make no mistake. Almost everybody admitted that they were "strong" and everybody shook their heads in amazement.

Yes, they were strong, and bold, and even audacious.

A wonderful audacity shown to the whole world!

I have repeated several times, all this was admitted "with amazement". And that was indeed how it was.

Power passed from the weak to the strong.

Strength always, at its very heart, gives birth to rapture.

And this rapture may be silent, and it may be felt only in the underground of the soul, but still—rapture.

Rapture at one's enemies? Can we really admit such a thing? And thus, it seems, in a very subtle way, amazement was born.

Amazement at one's enemies we can admit to. It is quite acceptable. But this is just an illusion. An optical illusion, an emotional trick. For the most part it was something else.

So, yes, there was amazement. Amazement at the strong hand, at the strongest desires of the strong. Amazement and fear, fear and rapture.

Do you remember how in those days a talented wit compared Russia to a woman? And her desire for slavish subjugation to a bold, brave lord and master?

Many will remember those words. And back then everybody shouted: "Yes, that's true. What a brilliant and true thought!" And they waited and waited for the power of the strongest and of the audacious. To swoon, to be destroyed under a strong hand, under the hiss of the whip raised above them.

If that is really the case, then the desires of this woman—Russia— have really come true.

The bloody scar on the back of the bourgeois is verily the mark of the strongest power, the mark of a wonderful audacity shown to the whole world.

So what do you want?

They were weak; and you cried, "Stronger!"

And now your wish is granted. Kiss the whip that is raised above you.

It's cruel, you say? Yes, but, on the other hand, it is powerful.

There is a lot of blood, you say?

Perhaps there is. Perhaps there is.

But then again, not so much that we shall drown in it....

PETROGRAD, 1918
(SIGNED WITH THE PSEUDONYM "MIKHAIL CHIRKOV")
(Translated by Rose France)

MIKHAIL BULGAKOV (1891–1940)

Future Prospects

Now, when our unhappy motherland finds itself at the very bottom of the pit of shame and hardship into which it has been driven by the "great socialist revolution", many of us are haunted by a single thought.

The thought is persistent.

Dark and gloomy, it looms in the consciousness, imperiously demanding a response.

The thought is simple enough: What will become of us?

It is a natural question.

We have analysed our recent past. Oh, how well we've studied each moment of the past two years. Not only have we studied these moments—a great many of us have cursed them.

Now we stand face-to-face with the present. And all we want to do is shut our eyes.

Don't make us see it!

All that remains is the future. An unknown, enigmatic future.

Indeed, what will become of us?...

Not long ago I had the chance to leaf through some issues of an English illustrated journal.

Enchanted, I gazed for a long time at the marvellous photographs.

Afterwards, for a long, long time, I simply pondered them, and then suddenly...

It all made sense! The picture was clear.

Day after day, colossal machines in colossal factories feverishly gobbling up coal, groaning, knocking, pouring out streams of molten metal, forging, fixing, building...

They are forging the might of the world. They have taken the place of those other machines, which had so recently sowed death and destruction, forging the might of victory.

In the West the great war of great peoples has ended. Now they are all licking their wounds.

They will, of course, get better. Quite soon they will feel much better!

And anyone whose mind has cleared, anyone who has rejected the pathetic, delirious notion that our virulent illness will spread to the West and infect it, will have no trouble perceiving this mighty surge of the world's titanic work—a surge that will lift the Western nations to unexampled heights of world power.

And what about us?

We... We will fall behind...

We'll fall so far behind that not a single living prophet could possibly tell us just when we'll finally manage to catch up—or whether we'll ever manage to catch up at all.

For we are being punished.

We cannot create. We have a grave task before us—to conquer and take back our own land.

They have begun to pay.

Heroic volunteers are tearing the Russian land from Trotsky's hands inch by inch.

And all of us, all of us—both those who perform their duty without hesitation, and those who hunker down in the southern cities, far from the front, telling themselves in their bitter delusion that they can contribute nothing to their nation's salvation—we all passionately await the liberation of our land.

And it will be liberated.

For every country has its heroes, and it is a crime to think that the motherland has perished.

But we shall have to fight a great deal, we shall have to shed much blood; for as long as the sinister figure of Trotsky leads his roving band of crazed, armed dupes, there can be no life—only a battle to the death.

We must fight.

And so, while over there the West resounds with the clatter of the machines of creation, our country resounds from end to end with the clatter of machine guns.

The insanity of the past two years has sent us down a frightening path without stops, without so much as a halt for breath. We have begun to drink from our cup of punishment, and we shall drink it to the dregs.

There, in the West, innumerable electric lights will glimmer. Pilots will pierce the conquered air. There they will build, research, print, study...

While we... We shall fight.

For no force can change that.

We are going to fight for our own capitals.

And we will win them back.

The English will recall how we had covered fields with bloody dew in our battle with Germany, how we drew the foes away from Paris; and they will lend us some more overcoats and boots so we can reach Moscow.

And reach Moscow we will.

The scoundrels and maniacs will be driven out, scattered, annihilated.

And the war will end.

Then our blood-soaked, demolished nation will start getting back on its feet... It will rise slowly, laboriously.

Alas, those who complain of "weariness" will be greatly disappointed. For they will have to grow "wearier" yet...

We shall have to pay for the past with unfathomable labour and with a life of harsh poverty. We shall have to pay in ways both figurative and literal.

We shall pay for the madness of those March days, for the madness of those October days, for the traitorous separatists, for the corruption of the workers, for Brest, for the insane use of machines to print money... for everything!

And we will pay it all off.

And only then, when it is very late indeed, shall we once again begin to create—so that we too regain our full rights, so that we too are welcome in the halls of Versailles.

Who will see those bright days?

Us?

No chance! Perhaps our children, or perhaps our grandchildren. For the scope of history is broad, and it "reads" decades as easily as a single year.

And we, the representatives of a failed generation, dying at the rank of pitiful paupers, shall have no choice but to tell our children, "Pay, pay honestly, and never forget the socialist revolution!"

13 NOVEMBER 1919
(Translated by Martha Kelly)

Notes

p. 8, *may be read alongside their volumes*: Orlando Figes, *A People's Tragedy: The Russian Revolution, 1891–1924* (London: Bodley Head, 2014); Sheila Fitzpatrick, *The Russian Revolution*, 2nd edn (Oxford: Oxford University Press, 2001); and Robert Service, *The Russian Revolution, 1900–1927*, 4th edn (London: Palgrave Macmillan, 2009). For a concise overview, see S.A. Smith, *The Russian Revolution: A Very Short Introduction* (Oxford: Oxford University Press, 2002). For an interesting reinterpretation of the period, see Jonathan Smele, *The 'Russian' Civil Wars, 1916–1926: Ten Years That Shook the World* (Oxford: Oxford University Press, 2016). Smele has also compiled an invaluable bibliography of English-language sources on the period, *The Russian Revolution and Civil War, 1917–1921: An Annotated Bibliography* (London and New York: Continuum, 2006). To get a sense of the variety of the Russian political landscape during the revolutionary period, see Michael C. Hickey, *Competing Voices from the Russian Revolution* (Santa Barbara, CA: Greenwood, 2011), and for a selection of popular reactions to the events of 1917, see Mark D. Steinberg, *Voices of Revolution, 1917*, trans. Marian Schwartz (New Haven: Yale University Press, 2001).

p. 15, *will continue to be destroyed*: Maxim Gorky, 'December 7 (20), 1917', in id., *Untimely Thoughts*, trans. Herman Ermolaev, 2nd rev. edn (New Haven: Yale University Press, 1995), p. 101.

p. 16, *But they needed order more*: Albert Rhys Williams, *Through the Russian Revolution* (New York: Boni and Liveright, 1921), p. 163. See also: Bessie Beatty, *The Red Heart of Russia* (New York: The Century Co., 1918), pp. 329–34; Louise Bryant, *Six Red Months in Russia: An Observer's Account of Russia Before and During the Proletarian Dictatorship* (New York: George H. Doran Company, 1918), pp. 158–59; and Michael Glenny and Norman Stone (eds.), *The Other Russia* (New York: Viking, 1991), p. 104.

p. 17, *an 'eloquent phrase' that can increase bloodshed*: Gorky, 'December 7 (20), 1917', p. 101.

p. 17, *the gallant loser, the victim*: Peter France, *Poets of Modern Russia* (Cambridge: Cambridge University Press, 1982), p. 143.

p. 17, *a political party or the state*: Simon Karlinsky, *Marina Tsvetaeva: The Woman, Her World, and Her Poetry* (Cambridge: Cambridge University Press, 1985), p. 67.

p. 18, *Left—it is 'right' in content*: Marina Tsvetaeva, letter to Anna Teskova, 1929, in Marina Tsvetaeva, *Sobranie sochinenii v semi tomakh*, ed. Anna Saakiants and Lev Mnukhin (Moscow: Ellis Lak, 1995), vol. 6, p. 385.

p. 19, *You stepped from a stately cathedral*: Tsvetaeva read this poem to Konstantin Balmont (1867–1942), one of the leading poets of the Symbolist movement, and recorded his response: "Balmont listened and replied, 'I don't like your disdain for the girl! I'm offended for her! Because the girl (eyes rolled back blissfully) is of a different kind...' I said, 'I'm sorry I can't say that the soldier, too, is of a different kind...'"

p. 22, *12 November 1917*: The Constituent Assembly, which was to decide who would govern Russia by democratic means, had indeed been the dream of liberal Russians for decades. Kerensky's Provisional Government wavered on the question of the assembly after the February Revolution, and the Bolsheviks used this reluctance as a justification for the October coup. The assembly elections were held on 12 (25) November, with the Socialist Revolutionary Party winning a majority of the vote and the Bolsheviks coming in a distant second. When the assembly was convened in January, the Bolsheviks—who had made an alliance with the Left faction of the Socialist Revolutionaries—had it dissolved; the Third All-Russian Congress of Soviets of Workers', Soldiers' and Peasants' Deputies, which was convened in place of the assembly, secured Bolshevik rule.

p. 23, *14 December 1917*: 14 (26) December was a date of great significance to Gippius and her husband, the Symbolist Dmitry Merezhkovsky (1866–1941), to whom this poem is dedicated. The date marks the anniversary of the Decembrist Uprising, in which a group of nobles in the clandestine 'Northern Society', including Valerian Golitsyn (1803–59), Sergey Trubetskoy (1790–1860), and the poet Kondraty Ryleyev (1795–1826), attempted to prevent the coronation of Tsar Nicholas I and establish a constitutional monarchy. After the Uprising was quelled, five of the participants, Ryleyev among them, were executed, while others were sent into exile in Siberia. In 1918, Merezhkovsky published a novel titled *14 December*—focusing on Golitsyn, a relatively minor figure in the Uprising—and the couple fled Soviet Russia on that date in 1919, eventually settling in Paris and becoming central figures in that 'capital' of the Russian emigration.

p. 24, *In public and behind closed doors...*: In Osip Mandelstam's symbolic geography, the Germanic north is associated with strength and masculinity while the Mediterranean South connotes civilization and refinement. This poem dramatizes the choice facing Russia—and the poet—at the end of 1917: Will the "maiden" accept the Rhine wine or soberly opt for

Southern air? It appears to be Mandelstam's hope that Russia will refuse the northern way, which is ultimately too crude and too joyless. But the temptation is itself intoxicating.

p. 25, *to mystical love or whatever else*: Sergey Gorodetsky, 'Nekotorye techeniia v sovremennoi russkoi poezii', *Apollon* 1 (1913), pp. 46–50 (p. 48), quoted in Robert Chandler, Boris Dralyuk and Irina Mashinski (eds.), *The Penguin Book of Russian Poetry* (London: Penguin Classics, 2015), p. 223. For more on the Acmeist doctrine, see Justin Doherty, *The Acmeist Movement in Russian Poetry: Culture and the Word* (Oxford: Clarendon Press, 1995).

p. 26, *Petrograd, Moscow, Crimea, Kiev and Tiflis*: For an account of Mandelstam's politics and peregrinations, see Clarence Brown, *Mandelstam* (Cambridge: Cambridge University Press, 1973), pp. 69–98.

p. 27, *her personal triumph and her generation's achievement*: For more on Akhmatova's life, see Elaine Feinstein, *Anna of All the Russias: The Life of Anna Akhmatova* (London: Weidenfeld & Nicolson, 2005).

p. 27, *clairvoyant and possessed of a soul*: Boris Pasternak, *Polnoe sobranie sochinenii s prilozheniiami v odinadtsati tomakh*, ed. E.B. Pasternak and E.V. Pasternak (Moscow: Slovo, 2004), vol. 3, p. 532. For more on Pasternak, see: Christopher Barnes, *Boris Pasternak: A Literary Biography*, 2 vols. (Cambridge: Cambridge University Press, 2004); and Lazar Fleishman, *Boris Pasternak: The Poet and His Politics* (Cambridge, MA: Harvard University Press, 1990).

p. 28, *May 1918, Moscow*: Mandelstam's poem, commemorating the first anniversary of the revolution, was originally published under the title '*Gimn*', which, to the Russian ear, suggests both solemn "hymn" and rousing "anthem". The striking ambiguity of that title permeates the entire work. The very first line presents a major problem for the reader, to say nothing of the translator; the Russian word *sumerki*, which is connected to liberty, generally means "twilight", but may also refer to the darkness before dawn; that rarer sense is triggered by the poem's markedly archaic rhetoric. So what, exactly, is Mandelstam asking us to praise—liberty's fading light, or its first faint glimmer? To preserve the ambiguity, I have rendered the word's first occurrence as "dim light". One may say that ambiguity is the very theme of Mandelstam's "hymn" to the revolution, reflected in a radical confusion of the elements (earth, water and air) and disorienting internal contradictions, like the leader's shouldering of an unbearable burden. This ambiguity contrasts sharply with—and is accentuated by—the poem's vigorous form and exalted tone. Attentive to the events of his time, Mandelstam reserves his judgement. As usual, he takes the long view: the world has been transformed at great cost, and though it may well have been worth it, we must not forget the expense. For an exhaustive reading of the poem, on which this note and translation relies, see Nils Åke Nilsson, *Osip Mandel'štam: Five Poems* (Stockholm: Almqvist & Wiksell International, 1974), pp. 47–68.

p. 32, *crowding the streets, thoroughly seduced him*: John E. Malmstad and Nikolay Bogomolov, *Mikhail Kuzmin: A Life in Art* (Cambridge, MA: Harvard University Press, 1999), pp. 253–54.

p. 33, *with male poets*: Gordon McVay's *Esenin: A Life* (Ann Arbor: Ardis, 1976) is the fullest biography of the poet in English. In *Isadora and Esenin* (Ann Arbor: Ardis, 1980), McVay discusses the poet's marriage to the dancer Isadora Duncan, as well as his potential bisexuality (pp. 30–32). For more on Esenin's, Klyuev's and Kuzmin's sexuality, and on the treatment of homosexuals in the Soviet period, see Simon Karlinsky, 'Russia's Gay Literature and Culture: The Impact of the October Revolution', in Martin

Bauml Duberman, Martha Vicinus and George Chauncey, Jr. (eds.), *Hidden from History: Reclaiming the Gay and Lesbian Past* (New York: New American Library, 1989), pp. 347–64.

p. 33, *and those of the intellectuals*: See Stefani Hoffman, 'Scythian Theory and Literature, 1917–1924', in Nils Åke Nilsson (ed.), *Art, Society, Revolution: Russia, 1917–21* (Stockholm: Almqvist & Wiksell International, 1979), pp. 138–64.

p. 34, *a kind of November*: McVay, *Esenin: A Life*, p. 204.

p. 39, *the political decadence of that class*: Leon Trotsky, *Literature and Revolution*, trans. Rose Strunsky, ed. and intro. William Keach (Chicago: Haymarket Books, 2005), p. 154. For more on Proletkult, see: Lynn Mally, *Culture of the Future: The Proletkult Movement in Revolutionary Russia* (Berkeley: University of California Press, 1990); and Mark D. Steinberg, *Proletarian Imagination: Self, Modernity, and the Sacred in Russia, 1910–1925* (Ithaca, NY: Cornell University Press, 2002).

p. 46, *most talented poet of our Soviet era*: Stalin wrote these words on a letter by Lili Brik (1891–1978), Mayakovsky's muse and tireless guardian of his legacy; they were printed in a front-page editorial in the 5 December 1935 issue of *Pravda*.

p. 46, *made that choice in his poetry*: Vladimir Mayakovsky, 'Alexander Blok Is Dead', in id., *Selected Works in Three Volumes*, ed. Alexander Ushakov (Moscow: Raduga Publishers, 1987), vol. 3, p. 166. The obituary first appeared in the newspaper *Agit-Rosta*, No. 14 (10 August 1921).

p. 47, *a new, harmonious way of life*: In a diary entry of 7 August 1917, Blok wrote: "Here is the *challenge facing Russian culture*—to direct this fire at that which needs to be burnt; to turn the riotous violence of Stenka [Razin] and Yemelka [Yemelyan Pugachov] into a wilful musical wave." Aleksandr Blok, *Sobranie sochinenii v vos'mi tomakh*, ed. V.N. Orlov, A.A. Surkov and K.I. Chukovskii (Moscow: Gosizdat, 1960–63), vol. 7, p. 297. His diary entry for 6 January 1919 justifies the destruction of his estate (see ibid., p. 353). See also Bernice Glatzer Rosenthal, 'Eschatology and the Appeal of Revolution: Merezhkovsky, Bely, Blok', *California Slavic Studies* 11 (1980), pp. 105–39.

p. 47, *extraordinary powers of intuition and observation*: See Avril Pyman, *A History of Russian Symbolism* (New York: Cambridge University Press, 1994).

p. 47, *if not go up in flames*: See Ben Hellman, *Poets of Hope and Despair: The Russian Symbolists in War and Revolution (1914–1918)* (Helsinki: Institute for Russian and East European Studies, 1995).

p. 48, *with every stirring of your conscience*: Alexander Blok, 'Intelligentsia and the Revolution', in id., *The Spirit of Music*, trans. I. Freiman (London: Lindsay Drummond Ltd., 1946), p. 20; for the original, see Aleksandr Blok, 'Intelligentsiia i revolutsiia', in id., *Sobranie sochinenii v vos'mi tomakh*, ed. V.N. Orlov, A.A. Surkov and K.I. Chukovskii (Moscow: Gosizdat, 1960–63), vol. 6, p. 20.

p. 48, *order with a grand anarchic sweep*: For a thorough analysis and contextualization of the poem, see Sergei Hackel's *The Poet and the Revolution: Aleksandr Blok's 'The Twelve'* (Oxford: Clarendon Press, 1975). See also Avril Pyman's notes to the poem in Avril Pyman (ed.), *Alexander Blok: Selected Poems* (Oxford: Pergamon Press, 1972), pp. 271–76.

p. 48, *His poem, The Twelve, will remain for ever*: Trotsky, *Literature and Revolution*, p. 111.

p.48, *likely a cerebral haemorrhage*: Gerald Janecek (ed.), *Andrey Bely: A Critical Review* (Lexington, Kentucky: The University of Kentucky Press, 1978), p. 8.

p. 49, *'Russia'*: This translation is drawn from a slim book called *Modern Poems from Russia* (London: G. Allen & Unwin, 1942), rendered by an Englishman named Gerard Shelley (1891–1980) and published when the wartime alliance with the Soviet Union opened new doorways for cultural exchange between Russia and the English-speaking world. Shelley mistranslates the first word, which should be "wail" (*ryday*); although the fiery thrust of Bely's rhetoric runs away with him, the results are appropriately forceful. According to his colourful but highly unreliable memoirs, *The Speckled Domes* and *The Blue Steppes*—both published in 1925—Shelley had spent the years 1913 through 1920 in Russia. He claims to have developed a friendship with the empress's notorious spiritual mentor and confidant, Grigory Rasputin, before winding up a prisoner of the Bolsheviks after the October Revolution. According to his account in *The Speckled Domes*, Shelley made a narrow escape to Finland disguised as a woman. Unfortunately, both his memoirs, and especially *The Blue Steppes*, are marred by egregious anti-Semitism, depicting the spread of communism as a Jewish conspiracy. The fact that many Jews, who had been systematically persecuted under the tsarist regime, participated in the revolutionary movement, be it as Bolsheviks, Mensheviks or Socialist Revolutionaries, is undeniable and, to some degree, self-explanatory; the notion that the revolutionaries' avowed ideology was merely a mask for a secret Jewish plot is, on the other hand, the stuff of anti-Semitic paranoia. See: André Gerrits, *The Myth of Jewish Communism: A Historical Interpretation* (Brussels: Peter Lang, 2009); and Oleg Budnitskii, *Russian Jews Between the Reds and the Whites, 1917–1920*, trans. Timothy J. Portice (Philadelphia: University of Pennsylvania Press, 2011).

p. 53, *should have diamonds on their backs*: In the imperial period, convicts sentenced to hard labour wore uniforms with diamonds on their backs; the Red Army men look and behave like hardened criminals—all they are missing is the diamond.

p. 53, *Kerensky roubles in her stocking*: Kerensky roubles, or "kerenkas", were the banknotes issued by the Provisional Government in 1917, named so after Alexander Kerensky; these notes were issued under Bolshevik rule until 1919.

p. 60, *Grant rest to the soul of Thy handmaiden, Lord*: This is a line from the Orthodox prayer for the dead.

p. 60, *roam without wine, my brothers*: This is a reference to the renewed ban on the sale of alcohol in revolutionary Petrograd. See 'Stolen Wine', pp. 15–18.

p. 63, *up ahead—is Jesus Christ*: In one of several similar notes, Blok wrote, "I do not like the end of *The Twelve* either. I would like its end to be different. When I finished the poem, I was amazed myself: Why Christ? But the more I looked into it, the more clearly I saw Christ. And, then and there, I made an entry: 'Unfortunately it has to be Christ.'" Blok, *Sobranie sochinenii*, vol. 3, p. 628.

p. 66, *O hear the summons of the barbarian lyre!*: In the third stanza, Blok alludes to the catastrophic earthquakes that levelled Lisbon in the fourteenth and eighteenth centuries, and the one that destroyed Messina in 1908. In the fifth stanza, he refers to the sacking of the Ancient Greek colony of Paestum, in what is now southern Italy, by Arabs in the ninth century. Though never a member of the Scythians (see p. 33), Blok was close to the group in the months following the October Revolution and, in this poem, gave clear expression to their ideology. The Allies' refusal to negotiate a peace with Germany and end the Great War infuriated Blok and prompted him to write the poem—a passionate, doom-laden ultimatum.

p. 67, *'Petersburg'*: Donald Rayfield writes about his translation:

> The future *Blue Horns* poet Titsian Tabidze was in his twenties heavily indebted to Russian poetry, especially Alexander Blok and Andrey Bely; but in 1917 he was abandoning their influence for his own new expressionist style. Although he and some other *Blue Horns* were not unfriendly to the Bolshevik cause – and later welcomed the invasion of Georgia in February 1921 – like most Georgian intellectuals and politicians in Russia, he reacted to the revolutions of 1917 by fleeing to Georgia in the hope of helping to restore his homeland's independence. This picture of October 1917 was, ironically, composed in the comfort of his hometown, Kutaisi. (His cousin Galaktion Tabidze, who actually stayed in Petrograd during the October Revolution, wrote introverted poems that focused exclusively on the poet's loneliness in a capital his fellow-countrymen had deserted.)

p. 68, *producing only a handful of poems*: 'At the Top of My Voice' is the title of Mayakovsky's last long poem, completed in January 1930, just months before his suicide on 14 April 1930.

p. 69, *and sat down to my studies*: Vladimir Mayakovsky, *I Myself*, trans. Alex Miller, in id., *Selected Works in Three Volumes*, ed. Alexander Ushakov (Moscow: Raduga Publishers, 1987), vol. 1, pp. 30–43 (p. 36).

p. 69, *'Slap in the Face of Public Taste'*: This slap has indeed resounded across the world; there is no shortage of monographs and articles devoted to the Futurist moment in Russian literature, but the most perceptive, clear-headed and readable source is still Vladimir Markov, *Russian Futurism: A History* (Berkeley: University of California Press, 1968); see his chapter on Hylaea, pp. 29–60. One of the tamer Hylaeans, the poet Benedikt Livshits (1886–1938), has also left a fascinating and vivid memoir of his Hylaean youth, *The One and a Half-Eyed Archer*, trans. John Bowlt (Newtonville, MA: Oriental Research Partners, 1977). My annotated translations of four Hylaean manifestos were published as *A Slap in the Face: Four Russian Futurist Manifestos* (Los Angeles: Insert Blanc Press, 2013); see 'Russian Futurist Manifestos and the Steamship of Modernity', *World Literature Today* (25 June 2013), <http://www.worldliteraturetoday. org/russian-futurist-manifestos-and-steamship-modernity> (accessed 27 June 2016). For Kruchenykh and Khlebnikov's *zaum* poetics, see Gerald Janecek, *Zaum: The Transrational Poetry of Russian Futurism* (San Diego: San Diego State University Press, 1996). For Khlebnikov, see *The Collected Works of Velimir Khlebnikov*, ed. Charlotte Douglas and Ronald Vroon, trans. Paul Schmidt, 3 vols. (Cambridge, MA: Harvard University Press, 1987–97).

p. 69, *Proletkult*: Bengt Jangfeldt, *Mayakovsky: A Biography*, trans. Harry D. Watson (Chicago: University of Chicago Press, 2014), pp. 102, 95–105 and *passim*. For more detail, see Bengt Jangfeldt, 'Russian Futurism, 1917–1919', in Nils Åke Nilsson (ed.), *Art, Society, Revolution: Russia 1917–21* (Stockholm: Almqvist & Wiksell International, 1979), pp. 106–37.

p. 70, *support for any concrete political line*: Jangfeldt, *Mayakovsky*, p. 102.

p. 78, *his excellent novella The Duel (1905)*: Alexander Kuprin, *The Duel*, trans. Josh Billings (Brooklyn, NY: Melville House Publishing, 2011).

p. 78, *with a romantic and heroical keynote*: D.S. Mirsky, *Contemporary Russian Literature (1881–1925)* (New York: Alfred A. Knopf, 1926), p. 123.

p. 78, *He is now a resident in France*: Ibid., p. 124.

p. 79, *plunge into an orgy of bloodshed*: Nicholas J.L. Luker, *Alexander Kuprin* (Boston: Twayne Publishers, 1978), p. 145.

p. 79, *only a distant reflection of war*: Ibid.

p. 80, *would be going up with him*: Valentin Kataev, *A Mosaic of Life: or, The Magic Horn of Oberon*, trans. Moira Budberg and Gordon Latta (London: Angus and Robertson, 1976), p. 283.

p. 80, *in the higher atmospheric strata*: Ibid., p. 286.

p. 81, *by Soviet forces in February 1920*: Ivan Bunin's diary, *Cursed Days* (first full pub. 1936), is an evocative document of the experience of the Russian Civil War from an anti-Bolshevik intellectual's perspective. It is available in Thomas Gaiton Marullo's translation (Chicago: Ivan R. Dee, 1998).

p. 82, *as are his late impressionistic autobiographies*: For an analysis of these late works, see Richard C. Borden, *The Art of Writing Badly: Valentin Kataev's Mauvism and the Rebirth of Russian Modernism* (Evanston, IL: Northwestern University Press, 1999).

p. 85, *and a pair of half-pood bombs*: A *pood* is an obsolete Russian unit of measure, roughly equivalent to 36 pounds.

p. 87, *the fifty-three miles to Arensburg*: Under Russian imperial rule, the town of Kuressaare, Estonia, was known as Arensburg.

p. 109, *their attention to the cultural front*: Many of the authors mentioned here were busy serving in the Red Army or on the Bolsheviks' side during the Civil War, either as soldiers, political commissars (Furmanov), front-line reporters (Babel, Ivanov) or guerrillas (Fadeyev). For more on the difficulties facing the Bolsheviks on the cultural front during the Civil War—including illiteracy among their supporters, paper shortages, and so on—see the essays by Peter Kenez, Jeffrey Brooks and others in Abbott Gleason, Peter Kenez and Richard Stites (eds.), *Bolshevik Culture: Experiment and Order in the Russian Revolution* (Bloomington, IN: Indiana University Press, 1989). A translation of Ivanov's *Armoured Train 14–69* can be found in Carl R. Proffer, Ellendea Proffer, Ronald Meyer and Mary Ann Szporluk (eds.), *Russian Literature of the Twenties: An Anthology* (Ann Arbor: Ardis, 1987). A translation of Furmanov's *Chapayev* can be found in Nicholas J.L. Luker (ed.), *From Furmanov to Sholokhov: An Anthology of the Classics of Socialist Realism* (Ann Arbor: Ardis, 1988). New translations of Isaac Babel's *Red Cavalry* and *Odessa Stories* are available from Pushkin Press. Alexander Chramoff's anthology *Flying Osip: Stories of New Russia*, trans. L.S. Friedland and J.R. Piroshnikoff (New York: International Publishers, 1925) provides a fascinating contemporaneous glimpse at the state of early Soviet fiction; it includes Lidiya Seyfullina's 'The Lawbreakers' (1922), a story of children left orphaned and homeless by the events of 1914–21.

p. 111, *a single, unstoppable, multi-voiced heroic mass*: The short novel is included in Luker (ed.), *From Furmanov to Sholokhov*; it was also released by International Publishers in 1935, in an effective anonymous translation. The novel was the subject of an important literary controversy between Yevgeny Zamyatin (see pp. 158–60), who dismissed it as a compilation of "rusty", "tinselled" literary clichés mustered for propagandistic purposes, and Dmitry Furmanov, who thought it artistically masterful and ideologically honest; their debate can be regarded as marking a crossroads in the evolution of "official" Soviet fiction, which would follow the direction of Serafimovich and Furmanov for decades to come. See: Proffer et al. (eds.), *Russian Literature of the Twenties*, pp. 529–41; and Edward J. Brown,

Russian Literature since the Revolution (Cambridge, MA: Harvard University Press, 1982), pp. 123–25.

p. 112, *so-called "Night of the Murdered Poets"*: For more Soviet Yiddish writing for this period, see Joseph Sherman (ed.), *From Revolution to Repression: Soviet Yiddish Writing, 1917–1952* (Nottingham: Five Leaves Publications, 2012). See also: David Shneer, *Yiddish and the Creation of Soviet Jewish Culture: 1918–1930* (Cambridge: Cambridge University Press, 2004); Kenneth B. Moss, *Jewish Renaissance in the Russian Revolution* (Cambridge, MA: Harvard University Press, 2009); Harriet Murav, *Music from a Speeding Train: Jewish Literature in Post-Revolution Russia* (Stanford, CA: Stanford University Press, 2011); Efraim Sicher, *Jews in Russian Literature after the October Revolution: Writers and Artists between Hope and Apostasy* (Cambridge: Cambridge University Press, 1995); and Maxim D. Shrayer (ed.), *An Anthology of Jewish-Russian Literature: Two Centuries of Dual Identity in Prose and Poetry, 1801–2001*, 2 vols. (Armonk, NY: M. E. Sharpe, 2007).

p. 113, *the tsar's enormous estate—Livadia*: The Livadia Palace in Crimea was a summer retreat for Tsar Nicholas II and the imperial family.

p. 122, *translations worthy of her canny and cutting prose*: Teffi, *Subtly Worded*, trans. Anne Marie Jackson, with Robert and Elizabeth Chandler, Clare Kitson, Irina Steinberg and Natalia Wase (London: Pushkin Press, 2014).

p. 123, *worked until her death in 1952*: Teffi's memoir of her escape from Russia was recently published as *Memories: From Moscow to the Black Sea*, trans. Robert and Elizabeth Chandler, Anne Marie Jackson and Irina Steinberg (New York: NYRB Classics, 2016; London: Pushkin Press, 2016).

p. 124, *there would be a new offensive*: On 18 June 1917 the Provisional Government launched a fresh attack on the Eastern Front, which led to massive Russian losses due to the extreme lack of morale among the Russian troops. The move played into Bolshevik hands.

p. 124, *with the term "tail-endism"*: Lenin himself coined this term to criticize non-Bolshevik Social Democrats in his article 'Two Tactics' (*Dve taktiki*), *Vpered*, No. 6 (14 February 1905).

p. 124, *caught napping by Gapon's movement*: Father Georgy Gapon (1870–1906) was a Russian Orthodox priest who advocated for workers' rights in St Petersburg before the Russian Revolution of 1905. On 9 January 1905, after the declaration of a general strike, he organized a peaceful march to present a petition to the tsar at the Winter Palace. Soldiers opened fire on the procession, killing hundreds. The events of this Bloody Sunday set off the revolution of 1905.

p. 126, *could explain why* agents provocateurs: The secret police of the tsarist regime, the Okhrana, had a policy of recruiting agents to infiltrate the Bolsheviks and other political parties in order to weaken and discredit them. Part of the activity of the *provocateurs* was to maintain the split between the Bolsheviks and Mensheviks.

p. 126, *utter tactlessness of the "sealed carriage"*: Lenin's clandestine journey back from neutral Switzerland in a sealed carriage was said to have been arranged—or at least supported—by the Germans, since it was in the Germans' interest to destabilize the tsarist regime.

p. 126, *Leninists, Bolsheviks, anarcho-communists, heavies, convicted housebreakers*: A reference to the tsarist *agent provocateur* Roman Malinovsky (see note to p. 127) and other Bolsheviks with criminal or otherwise questionable backgrounds.

p. 127, *memorable night after the Milyukov note*: In May 1917, the Provisional Government sent a secret telegram to the Allies informing them of Russia's intention to remain in the war. The "Milyukov note", as it became known, swelled support for the radical opposition.

p. 127, *the "reactionary hydra"*: The idea of the "reactionary hydra" was a common slogan at the time. Caricatured depictions of this many-headed monster appeared in radical propaganda.

p. 127, *He is even content with Malinovsky*: One of the most famous *agents provocateurs* was Roman Malinovsky (1876–1918), a former convicted criminal who turned police spy and managed to come to prominence in the Bolshevik Party. Lenin continued to support Malinovsky even after the latter was unmasked and forced to leave the country.

p. 131, *Guillotin, / Médecin, / Politique*: This popular song was sung to a famous minuet by Exaudet:

> *Guillotin,*
> *Médecin,*
> *Politique,*
> *Imagine, un beau matin,*
> *Que pendre est inhumain,*
> *Et peu patriotique.*
> *[...]*
> *Et sa main*
> *Fait soudain*
> *Une machine*
> *Humainement qui tuera*
> *Et qu'on appelera*
> *Guillotine.*

[Guillotin, a doctor and a politician, imagines, one fine morning, that to hang people is inhuman and unpatriotic. [...] So his hand, all of a sudden, makes a machine that will kill humanely, which we will call the guillotine.]

p. 131, *"Monsieur de Paris"*: Charles-Henri Sanson—the royal executioner in France under Louis XVI, and later state executioner of the First Republic, who guillotined the king himself—was known by this title.

p. 131, *You can wave my head goodbye!*: *Chastushki* were four-line popular songs, usually topical and with a satirical content, that could be adapted to reflect the current situation and the political sympathies of the singer. Though this urban folkloric genre dates back to the 1860s, it is now commonly associated with the communists and the Red Army; however, many popular *chastushki* express anti-Soviet sentiment.

p. 133, *All I have is a million-rouble note*: Following the October Revolution, inflation, which had been gathering pace in Russia since February 1917, became still more rapid. At the time Teffi wrote this story, in 1918, there was no one-million-rouble note, but the story is set in the near future and her prediction was borne out: the one-million-rouble note was actually introduced in 1921.

p. 133, *told us to "break a leg"*: The cab driver in the Russian story wishes the friends "gentle steam"—the standard Russian wish when somebody is about to go for a steam bath.

p. 133, *together with vendors of* sbiten: A traditional Russian drink, mentioned in sources dating back to the twelfth century, made of water, honey, spices and jam. It is served hot in the winter.

p. 136, *from their native Betluga to Simbirsk*: In 1924 Simbirsk was renamed Ulyanovsk, in honour of its most famous citizen, Lenin, whose real surname was Ulyanov. It also happened to be Kerensky's home town.

p. 137, *pious and blasphemous, philo- and anti-Semitic*: The past few decades have seen a resurgence of interest in Rozanov, evidenced by a spate of English-language book-length studies, including: Anna Lisa Crone's *Rozanov and the End of Literature: Polyphony and the Dissolution of Genre in Solitaria and Fallen Leaves* (Wurzburg: Jal-Verlag, 1978); Henrietta Mondry's *Vasily Rozanov and the Body of Russian Literature* (Bloomington, IN: Slavica, 2010); and Adam Ure's *Vasilii Rozanov and the Creation: The Edenic Vision and the Rejection of Eschatology* (London and New York: Continuum, 2011).

p. 138, *which he founded in 1907*: For more on this society and Remizov's eccentricity, see Julia Friedman, *Beyond Symbolism and Surrealism: Alexei Remizov's Synthetic Art* (Evanston, IL: Northwestern University Press, 2010), pp. 16–17. Friedman's book is an excellent introduction to Remizov's work, as is Greta N. Slobin's *Remizov's Fictions, 1900–1921* (DeKalb, IL: Northern Illinois University Press, 1991).

p. 138, *and alone in our wandering life*: Aleksei Remizov, 'Tri mogily', in id., *Sobranie sochinenii v desiati tomakh* (Moscow: Russkaia kniga, 2000), vol. 5, pp. 226–27 (p. 227). Remizov's memoir, *Kukkha: Rozanovy pis'ma*, is included in vol. 7 of the *Sobranie sochinenii*, pp. 31–132.

p. 138, *poet comes to a different conclusion*: See Hackel, *The Poet and the Revolution*, pp. 165–77.

p. 140, *into something like the "Polabian Slavs"*: The Polabian Slavs settled along the Elbe River in what is now Germany in the sixth century and were conquered by the Saxons and Danes in the ninth century. All but the Sorbs, one of the three main Polabian tribes, whose descendants now number some sixty thousand, were Germanized in the twelfth century.

p. 143, *first at Ciniselli Circus, then at Tsarskoe Selo*: Maria Dolina (1868–1919) was a contralto who toured Western Europe and Russia before the revolution, performing Russian and Slavic lieder and folk songs. The ornate, brick-built Ciniselli Circus, which opened in 1877, still stands in St Petersburg.

p. 144, *Leonid Andreyev had nothing to spit out*: Leonid Andreyev (1871–1919) was a leading prose author of the Silver Age of Russian literature, whose works combined elements of Naturalism and Symbolism.

p. 146, *you in dream and in waking*: The myth of St Petersburg is forever bound with Étienne Maurice Falconet's 1782 equestrian monument to the city's founder, Peter the Great. The Bronze Horseman was first brought to life in Alexander Pushkin's eponymous epic poem of 1833, and it has continued to haunt the imagination of Russia's authors.

p. 147, *was not to be endured*: In 1598, the death of Fyodor Ivanovich, Ivan the Terrible's son and the last member of the Rurik dynasty, plunged Russia into chaos until the first Romanov, Mikhail, was elected tsar in 1613. During this so-called Time of Troubles, a number of impostors came forward, claiming to be Ivan's other son, Dmitry, who had actually been killed in 1591. Only the first of these three False Dmitrys managed to rise to the throne in 1605–06, but the other two wreaked significant havoc until 1612.

p. 147, *There was a Cain in Rus*: Vanka Kain (né Ivan Osipov, 1718–c.1756), whose moniker alludes to the Biblical Cain, was a notorious Russian bandit and member of the Moscow police. Tales chronicling his exploits were extraordinarily popular in the eighteenth and nineteenth centuries, and often included songs reputedly composed by Kain himself. See David Gasperetti's annotated translation of Matvei Komarov's *Vanka Kain* (1779) in *Three Russian Tales of the Eighteenth Century: The Comely Cook, Vanka Kain, and Poor Liza*, trans. and intro. David Gasperetti (DeKalb, IL: Northern Illinois University Press, 2012).

p. 147, *'twas near Trinity, near Sergey*: The Trinity Lavra of St Sergius is Russian Orthodoxy's holiest site. It is located in the town of Sergiyev Posad, where Rozanov spent the last year and a half of his life.

p. 149, *the boundless Gogolian steppes*: The early stories of Ukrainian–Russian writer Nikolay Gogol (1809–52), one of the first true masters of Russian prose, were set in the steppes of Ukraine and abounded in fantastic elements, including ghosts and evil spirits.

p. 151, *heaven was rolled up like a scroll*: This alludes to Revelation 6:14.

p. 152, *there is nothing*: Kitezh is a mythical submerged city. According to an eighteenth-century manuscript called the *Kitezh Chronicle*, the city sank beneath the waves of Lake Svetloyar in Central Russia in order to escape being sacked by Batu Khan's troops in the thirteenth century.

p. 154, *"E-ter-nal me-mo-ry..."*: "Eternal memory" (*vechnaia pamiat'*) are the words uttered at the end of a Russian Orthodox funeral or memorial service.

p. 157, *the very soul of the Revolution*: Alexander Berkman, *The Bolshevik Myth (Diary, 1920–22)* (New York: Boni & Liveright, 1925), pp. 90–91.

p. 158, *abolished, when they have become unnecessary*: Ibid., pp. 97–98.

p. 159, *for many years under tsarist rule*: In his *Literature and Revolution*, Trotsky calls him an "internal émigré" (Trotsky, *Literature and Revolution*, p. 43). For more on the House of Arts and the Serapions, whose ranks included Vsevolod Ivanov (1895–1963), Konstantin Fedin (1892–1977), Yelizaveta Polonskaya (née Movshenson, 1890–1969), Veniamin Kaverin (1902–89), Lev Lunts (1901–24), Viktor Shklovsky (1893–1984) and Mikhail Zoshchenko (see pp. 202–05), see: Hongor Oulanoff, *The Serapion Brothers: Theory and Practice* (The Hague: Mouton, 1966); Gary Kern and Christopher Collins (eds.), *The Serapion Brothers: A Critical Anthology* (Ann Arbor: Ardis, 1975); Leslie Dorfman Davis, *Serapion Sister: The Poetry of Elizaveta Polonskaja* (Evanston, IL: Northwestern University Press, 2001); and Martha Weitzel Hickey, *The Writer in Petrograd and the House of Arts* (Evanston, IL: Northwestern University Press, 2009).

p. 160, *in intensity from year to year*: Yevgeny Zamyatin, *The Dragon: Fifteen Stories*, trans. Mirra Ginsburg (Chicago: University of Chicago Press, 1976), p. xiii. Ginsburg also translated and edited a collection of Zamyatin's fascinating literary and cultural essays: Yevgeny Zamyatin, *A Soviet Heretic: Essays by Yevgeny Zamyatin* (Evanston, IL: Northwestern University Press, 1992).

p. 183, *to power and was eventually executed*: See: Aleksandr Voronsky, *Art as the Cognition of Life: Selected Writings, 1911–1936*, ed. and trans. Frederick S. Choate (Oak Park, MI: Mehring Books, 1998); and Brown, *Russian Literature since the Revolution*, pp. 153–66.

p. 183, Jen Sheng *became an international success*: The English edition of *Jen Sheng: The Root of Life*, in a translation by George Walton and Philip Gibbons, appeared from G.P. Putnam in 1936.

p. 183, *to subdue his magnificent, riddle-filled environment*: Mikhail Prishvin, *Nature's Diary*, trans. L. Navrozov (London: Penguin Books, 1987), p. xi.

p. 186, *generations of Soviet children and adolescents*: Nicholas J.L. Luker has been Grin's greatest champion in the Anglophone world, writing a number of articles on his work, as well as two full-length studies, *Alexander Grin* (Letchworth: Bradda Books, 1973) and *Aleksandr Grin: The Forgotten Visionary* (Newtonville, MA: Oriental Research Partners, 1980), and a volume of translations, *Selected Short Stories* (Ann Arbor: Ardis Publishers, 1987).

p. 188, *gone bust trading in Livny accordions*: A special accordion from the area around Livny in Central Russia, used by Russian folk musicians since the late nineteenth century.

p. 192, *keeps muttering something about Metropolitan Antony*: The Cross of St George was an important Imperial Russian military decoration, established in 1807 and abolished after the Bolshevik revolution. It was reinstated by the Russian government in 1992. Metropolitan Antony (né Alexey Pavlovich Khrapovitsky, 1863–1936) was a Russian Orthodox bishop instrumental in re-establishing the Moscow Patriarchate after the February Revolution; after the Bolshevik revolution he left for what is now Ukraine, served as Metropolitan of Kiev and Galicia (1918–20) and then left for Serbia, where he helped establish the Russian Orthodox Church Outside Russia (ROCOR).

p. 193, *that's awake, just twiddling his thumbs*: The Smolny compound, a part of which had previously served as an educational institute for young noblewomen, was the first headquarters of the Bolshevik regime.

p. 196, *Count Eugène Salias's collected works*: Count Eugène Salias de Tournemire (1840–1908) was a prolific and enormously successful author of historical fiction, dubbed the "Russian Dumas"; his collected works, published some years before the end of his career, consist of thirty-three volumes.

p. 199, *by amorous school children*: Nikolay Nekrasov (1821–78) was Russia's most influential poet of the 1860s and 1870s, whose socially critical verse continued to inspire generations of liberals and radicals.

p. 201, *abandoning the drug for good in 1918*: Hugh Aplin's translation of the doctor tales, as well as the story 'Morphine' (1927), which drew on Bulgakov's experiences with the drug, appears in *A Young Doctor's Notebook* (London: Alma Classics, 2011).

p. 202, *was Bulgakov's literary debut*: For an account of Bulgakov's activities during the Civil War and his first literary efforts, see Edythe C. Haber, *Mikhail Bulgakov: The Early Years* (Cambridge, MA: Harvard University Press, 1998), pp. 11–41.

p. 202, *at the Moscow Art Theatre throughout the 1930s*: Stalin made these remarks at a meeting with a group of Ukrainian authors on 12 February 1929, a record of which can be found in vol. twelve of the General Secretary's *Sochineniia* (Moscow: Gospolitizdat, 1951), p. 112; see also ibid., vol. 11, pp. 328–29.

p. 203, *We need rye bread, not brie cheese*: Mikhail and Vera Zoshchenko, *Neizdannyi Zoshchenko*, ed. Vera von Wiren (Ann Arbor: Ardis, 1976), p. 112. Marietta Chudakova argues that the piece described in *Before Sunrise* was a story sent together with this feuilleton, which has not survived (*Izbrannye raboty*, vol. 1: *Literatura sovetskogo proshlogo* [Moscow: Iazyki russkoi kul'tury, 2001], p. 82).

p. 203, *in his autobiography, Before Sunrise*: This penetrating, self-psycho-analytic autobiography has been translated by Gary Kern as *Before Sunrise: A Novella* (Ann Arbor: Ardis, 1974).

p. 204, *time in which they were written*: Zoshchenko, *Neizdannyi Zoshchenko*, p. 112.

p. 204, *he sensed a liking for him*: Ibid., p. 64.

p. 207, *strong power, ruthless towards its enemies*: The references are to Alexander Kuprin (see pp. 77–80) and Vladimir (né Natan) Bogoraz (1865–1936), a Russian Jewish Socialist Revolutionary activist, writer and pioneering ethnologist, who published creative work under the pseudonym N.A. Tan.

p. 208, *a bold, brave lord and master*: The reference is to Vasily Rozanov (see pp. 136–39).

Pushkin Press

Pushkin Press was founded in 1997, and publishes novels, essays, memoirs, children's books—everything from timeless classics to the urgent and contemporary.

Our books represent exciting, high-quality writing from around the world: we publish some of the twentieth century's most widely acclaimed, brilliant authors such as Stefan Zweig, Marcel Aymé, Teffi, Antal Szerb, Gaito Gazdanov and Yasushi Inoue, as well as compelling and award-winning contemporary writers, including Andrés Neuman, Edith Pearlman, Eka Kurniawan and Ayelet Gundar-Goshen.

Pushkin Press publishes the world's best stories, to be read and read again. Here are just some of the titles from our long and varied list. To discover more, visit www.pushkinpress.com.

THE SPECTRE OF ALEXANDER WOLF
GAITO GAZDANOV

'A mesmerising work of literature' Antony Beevor

SUMMER BEFORE THE DARK
VOLKER WEIDERMANN

'For such a slim book to convey with such poignancy the extinction of a generation of "Great Europeans" is a triumph' *Sunday Telegraph*

MESSAGES FROM A LOST WORLD
STEFAN ZWEIG

'At a time of monetary crisis and political disorder... Zweig's celebration of the brotherhood of peoples reminds us that there is another way' *The Nation*

BINOCULAR VISION
EDITH PEARLMAN

'A genius of the short story' Mark Lawson, *Guardian*

IN THE BEGINNING WAS THE SEA
TOMÁS GONZÁLEZ

'Smoothly intriguing narrative, with its touches of sinister, Patricia Highsmith-like menace' *Irish Times*

BEWARE OF PITY
STEFAN ZWEIG

'Zweig's fictional masterpiece' *Guardian*

THE ENCOUNTER
PETRU POPESCU

'A book that suggests new ways of looking at the world and our place within it' *Sunday Telegraph*

WAKE UP, SIR!
JONATHAN AMES

'The novel is extremely funny but it is also sad and poignant, and almost incredibly clever' *Guardian*

THE WORLD OF YESTERDAY
STEFAN ZWEIG

'*The World of Yesterday* is one of the greatest memoirs of the twentieth century, as perfect in its evocation of the world Zweig loved, as it is in its portrayal of how that world was destroyed' David Hare

WAKING LIONS
AYELET GUNDAR-GOSHEN

'A literary thriller that is used as a vehicle to explore big moral issues. I loved everything about it' *Daily Mail*

BONITA AVENUE
PETER BUWALDA

'One wild ride: a swirling helix of a family saga... a new writer as toe-curling as early Roth, as roomy as Franzen and as caustic as Houellebecq' *Sunday Telegraph*

JOURNEY BY MOONLIGHT
ANTAL SZERB

'Just divine... makes you imagine the author has had private access to your own soul' Nicholas Lezard, *Guardian*

BEFORE THE FEAST

SAŠA STANIŠIĆ

'Exceptional... cleverly done, and so mesmerising from
the off... thought-provoking and energetic' *Big Issue*

A SIMPLE STORY

LEILA GUERRIERO

'An epic of noble proportions... [Guerriero] is a mistress
of the telling phrase or the revealing detail' *Spectator*

FORTUNES OF FRANCE

ROBERT MERLE

1 *The Brethren*
2 *City of Wisdom and Blood*
3 *Heretic Dawn*

'Swashbuckling historical fiction' *Guardian*

TRAVELLER OF THE CENTURY

ANDRÉS NEUMAN

'A beautiful, accomplished novel: as ambitious as it is generous,
as moving as it is smart' Juan Gabriel Vásquez, *Guardian*

ONE NIGHT, MARKOVITCH

AYELET GUNDAR-GOSHEN

'Wry, ironically tinged and poignant... this is a fable
for the twenty-first century' *Sunday Telegraph*

KARATE CHOP & MINNA NEEDS REHEARSAL SPACE

DORTHE NORS

'Unique in form and effect... Nors has found a novel
way of getting into the human heart' *Guardian*

**RED LOVE: THE STORY OF AN EAST GERMAN
FAMILY**

MAXIM LEO

'Beautiful and supremely touching... an unbearably poignant
description of a world that no longer exists' *Sunday Telegraph*

SONG FOR AN APPROACHING STORM

PETER FRÖBERG IDLING

'Beautifully evocative... a must-read novel' *Daily Mail*

THE RABBIT BACK LITERATURE SOCIETY
PASI ILMARI JÄÄSKELÄINEN

'Wonderfully knotty... a very grown-up fantasy masquerading as quirky fable. Unexpected, thrilling and absurd' *Sunday Telegraph*

STAMMERED SONGBOOK: A MOTHER'S BOOK OF HOURS
ERWIN MORTIER

'Mortier has a poet's eye for vibrant detail and prose to match... If this is a book of fragmentation, it is also a son's moving tribute' *Observer*

BARCELONA SHADOWS
MARC PASTOR

'As gruesome as it is gripping... the writing is extraordinarily vivid... Highly recommended' *Independent*

THE LIBRARIAN
MIKHAIL ELIZAROV

'A romping good tale... Pretty sensational' *Big Issue*

WHILE THE GODS WERE SLEEPING
ERWIN MORTIER

'A monumental, phenomenal book' *De Morgen*

BUTTERFLIES IN NOVEMBER
AUÐUR AVA ÓLAFSDÓTTIR

'A funny, moving and occasionally bizarre exploration of life's upheavals and reversals' *Financial Times*

BY BLOOD
ELLEN ULLMAN

'Delicious and intriguing' *Daily Telegraph*

THE LAST DAYS
LAURENT SEKSIK

'Mesmerising... Seksik's portrait of Zweig's final months is dignified and tender' *Financial Times*

TALKING TO OURSELVES
ANDRÉS NEUMAN

'This is writing of a quality rarely encountered... when you read Neuman's beautiful novel, you realise a very high bar has been set' *Guardian*